Cooking With Shea

A collection of recipes from around Australia

Compiled by

Shea Gordon

Cooking With Shea

All Rights Reserved

Copyright © 2019 Shea Gordon

Reproduction in any manner, in whole or in part,
in English or any other language, or otherwise,
without the written permission of the copyright holder is
prohibited

For information address mickiedaltonbooks@lycos.com

First Printing 2019

ISBN: 978-0-6484766-9-6

Published by The Mickie Dalton Foundation
NSW
Australia

I am dedicating this Cook Book to my very beautiful and talented sister, SUSAN PATRICIA BROWN (WHITTER) who was trained by Margaret Fulton. Susan produced many Cook Books including books with Curtis Stone, Janice Baker and Charmaine Solomon.

Australian Cinematographers Society

VALE : Susan Brown (Whitter) - Food Stylist, Film and Print Media
In loving memory of Susan Brown (Whitter) who passed away Wednesday 13th June 2018 at 7.00am.

Susan's name is synonymous with food styling, being a leading Food Stylist in Australia for decades, having been flown for work overseas and around the country.

Susan, as a teenager during the mid 1970s, while studying at East Sydney Technical College for a Home Economics Certificate, was hand picked by Margaret Fulton to be her assistant at Woman's Day Magazine where Margaret was the Food Editor, once she had completed her studies.

Susan would assist Margaret testing and developing recipes in the testing kitchen of Woman's Day for the weekly editorial, the Margaret Fulton Cookbooks and the Margaret Fulton Cookery Course. Susan also assisted Margaret's sister Jean Hatfield at Woman's World.

Susan then took time off from her career to start and bring up her family.

Around 1980 Susan started her freelance career working with her good friend Janice Baker on the Complete Book of Baking for Lansdown Press photographed by Ray Joyce. From there it was then a natural progression, for someone as dedicated and passionate about food as Susan, into live action in the late 1980s.

Over the decades of live action television commercials, Susan also continued her work on stills shoots, cookbooks, editorials and days on the occasional feature film.

From the day Susan entered the film industry she began establishing her long-standing relationships with Multi-National Food Companies.

Susan's clients over the decades, to name just a few, have included:

KFC
Dominos
Continental Foods
Unifoods including Nestle
Pizza Hut
Canadian Tourist Bureau
Cadbury
Sara Lee
Streets
Blue Ribbon
McDonalds
Kelloggs
Safcol Tuna
Red Rooster
Pampas Pastry
Maggi
Hungry Jacks
Bulla
Yoplait
Coon Cheese
Various dog and cat foods
And working with world-renowned chef Curtis Stone on the Coles campaign

Susan also often worked closely, hand-in-hand, with model makers and standby props from around the world (and especially in Australia) over the decades to achieve the final desired product that ended up on our screens.

The Production Companies, Directors, Producers, Cinematographers and Stills Photographers Susan has worked with are too many to note as are the current food stylists Susan has inspired with her beautiful food imagery, loyalty, dedicated work ethic and passion for food.

Susan retired from the film industry in August of 2017.

Susan is survived by her much loved family; husband Mark, children Madeleine and Michael and her grandchildren. Family was everything to Susan, including her film industry family.

Susan's wish was for her funeral to be a happy occasion celebrating her life and for those attending to wear bright colours.

In lieu of flowers, Susan and Mark have requested that donations made to:

Blue Knot Foundation - for survivors of childhood trauma and abuse

link below - there is a donate button on the home page or go to 'Get Involved' option

https://www.blueknot.org.au/

Contents

Beef Recipes — 1

Shea's Cottage Pie	2
Shea's Beef Recipe	4
American Spare Ribs	5
Shea's Osso Bucco	6
Martina's Farmhouse Casserole	7
Farmhouse Casserole	8
Martina's Corned Beef	9
Martina's Corn Meat	10
Glazed Corn Beef	11
White Sauce	12
Shea's Corned Beef Silverside	13
BBQ Ribs	14
American Spare Ribs – No. 2	15
Quick Conversion Guide	16
Shea's Perfect Steak	17
Homestead Meatloaf	19
Healthy Meatloaf	20
Shea's Classic Meatloaf	22
Classic Meatloaf	24

Cakes and Sweets Recipes — 27

Rocky Road	28
Anzac Biscuits	29
Shea's Orange Date Muffins	30
Jo Woulfe's Banana Cake	31
Chris' Banana Bread	32
Cherry Crumble Recipe	33

Cakes and Sweets Recipes (Cont.)

Fudgy Chocolate Cake	34
Rosemary Feta and Walnut Damper	36
Triple Treat Biscuits	37

Chicken Recipes — 39

Shea's Roast Chicken	40
Chicken Maryland	41
Shea's Braised Chicken Leg	41
Chicken Marengo	43
Chicken Marengo (2)	44
Chicken Cutlets – Oven Baked	45
Roast Chicken with Couscous	47
Chicken Cutlets in a Baccarat Dutch Oven	48
Dutch Oven Baked Chicken Thighs	49
Lemon Grilled Chicken	51
Turkey Leg Roast	53
Shea's Roast Duck	54
Roast Duck	55
Roast Duck 2	59
BBQ Duck with Noodles	60

Curries — 61

Beef Curry	62
Madras Beef Curry	63
Indian Chicken Curry	64
Shea's Lamb Curry	65
Shea's Curried Sausages	66
Chicken Curry	67

Fish Recipes   69

    Shea's Baked Trout   70

    Pickled Herrings   71

    Fish Cakes   72

    Jamie Oliver's Fabulous Fish Cakes   73

    Crisp Honey Prawns   74

Italian Food   77

    Shea's Pizza   78

    Shea's Lasagna   79

    Tuna Pasta Bake   80

    Tomato, Spinach & Bocconina Pizza   81

Lamb Recipes   83

    Shea's Roast Lamb Shoulder   84

    Pot Roasted Lamb Shanks   86

    Shea's Roast Lamb 1.5 kilos   87

    Shea's Roast Lamb 2.7 kilos   89

    Braised Lamb Shoulder Chops   90

    Plumb & Rosemary Lamb Shanks   91

    Braised Lamb Shanks   92

    Baked Lamb Chops "Italian"   93

    Lamb Ragout   98

    Roast Leg of Lamb with Gravy   99

Pork Recipes   101

    Australian Port Roast Leg   102

    Shea's Roast Pork   103

    Rosemary Roasted Pork   104

    Shea's Pork Hocks   105

    Glazed Ham   106

Pebble Creek – Pork Leg Roast	109
Puffed Pastry Parcels	110

Soups   111

Shea's Ham & Beef Bones Soup	112
Shea's Pork Soup with Chinese Yam	113
Shea's Pork Soup with Four Chinese Herbs	114
Shea's Pork Soup with Lotus Seeds	115
Shea's Chicken and Cream Corn Soup	117
Hearty Chicken & Vegetable Soup	117
Stocks	118
Pumpkin Soup	120
Pea & Ham Soup	122

Special Health Foods   123

Boiling Vegetable	124
Danny's Delicious Salad	125
Mushroom and White Wine Risotto	126
Mushroom & Rosemary Risotto	127
Maple Syrup Glaze	128
Roasted Potato Medley	129
Salad Nicoise	130
Roasted Pumpkin	132
Anti-Cholesterol	134
Anti-Cancer Foods	136
Alkalizing Foods	137
Acidifying Foods	138
Anti-Inflammatory Foods	139
Dietary Fibre Guide	141
June Fresh – the bounty of fresh winter vegetables	139

God's Pharmacy — 145

- Carrots — 146
- Tomatoes — 147
- Walnuts — 147
- Grapes — 148
- Kidney Beans — 148
- Celery/Bok Choy/Rhubarb — 149
- Figs — 149
- Onions — 150
- Oranges — 150
- Avocados/Egg Plants/Pears — 151
- Olives — 151
- Sweet Potatoes — 152

Cooking With Shea

BEEF RECIPES

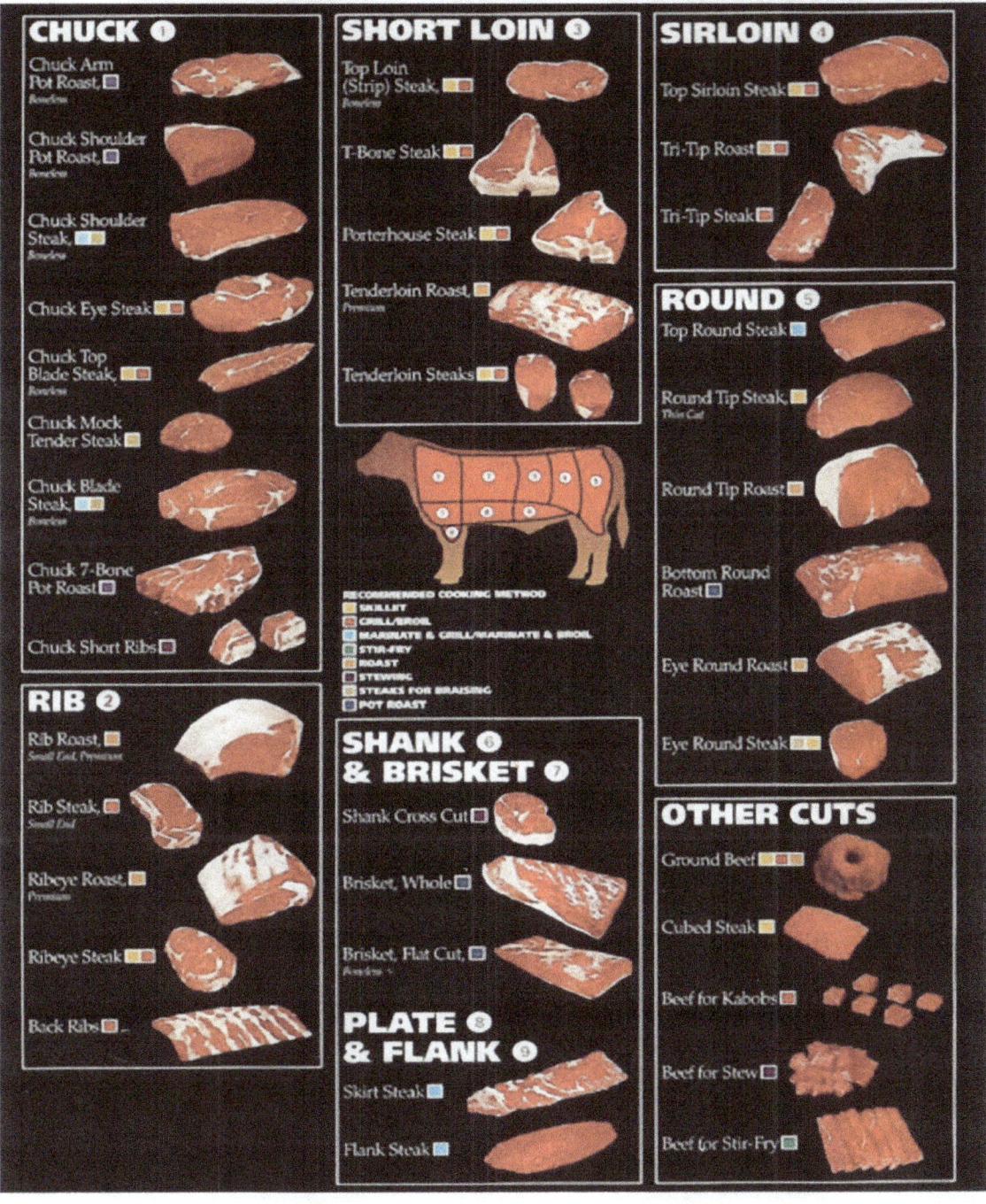

Cooking With Shea

SHEA'S COTTAGE PIE

Ingredients

2	TABLESPOONS OLIVE OIL
1	MEDIUM SIZED ONION FINELY CHOPPED
500GRAMS	BEEF MINCE
1	LARGE CARROT CHOPPED FINELY
1	MEDIUM ZUCCHINI FINELY CHOPPED
1/3	SMALL EGGPLANT FINELY CHOPPED
5	ROSETTES OF BROCCOLI FINELY CHOPPED
2	MUSHROOMS FINELY SLICED
2	GARLIC CLOVES FINELY CHOPPED
1	HANDFUL OF FRESH OREGANO FINELY CHOPPED
1	SMALL HANDFUL OF BASIL FINELY CHOPPED
1	440G TIN OF TOMATOES
2	TABLESPOONS OF TOMATO PASTE OR TOMATO SAUCE
½ CUP	RED WINE
½ CUP	MILK
40G	KERRYS GOLD BUTTER
750G	CREAM ROYALE POTATOES
¾ CUP	SHREDDED OR GRATED CHEESE

Cooking With Shea

Heat oil in pan.

Add Onion, Mushrooms, Eggplant.

Stir with Wooden Spoon until soft.

Add Beef Mince and stir until brown.

Add Carrot, Zucchini, Oregano, Basil, Broccoli, Garlic.

Stir with Wooden Spoon until soft.

Add Tinned Tomatoes, Tomato Paste or Sauce, Red Wine.

Stir to combine.

Cover and Simmer for 15 minutes or until vegetables are tender.

Meanwhile cook potatoes in a large saucepan of boiling water until tender.

Drain and then return saucepan over low heat. Mash. Stir in milk and butter.

Remove from heat.

Spoon mince mixture into 1.8 litre Pyrex Dish ovenproof.

Top with Mashed Potato with a spoon.

Sprinkle with shredded cheese all over the top.

Bake for 20 minutes or until golden brown.

Important: Preheat Convection Oven 200°C or Fan Forced 180°C.

Shea's Beef Recipe

INGREDIENTS

1 ½ kilo - Piece of Beef
Rosemary and Thyme and Oil Mixed Together
Or
Wholegrain Mustard and Oil Mixed Together
Plum Jam and Honey

METHOD

Preheat Oven to 180 ℃
Rub seasoning all over the top of Beef
Cook Beef for 25 to 30 minutes per 500g
Rest Beef for 15 minutes – cover with alfoil

Yorkshire Pudding Mixture

300ml Full Fat Milk,

1 Egg,

100g Plain Flour,

Pinch of Salt,

Vegetable Oil

American Spare Ribs

Ingredients

Ribs
Moroccan Paste
Honey
Thyme
Pepper

Lay Ribs Flat on Pyrex Oven Dish
Using pastry brush spread Moroccan Paste
over the Ribs
then
Sprinkle with Pepper
then
Sprinkle with Thyme
Then
Drizzle With Honey

Oven Temperature 160°c

Bake for 30 to 40 minutes (small rib)
Bake for 60 minutes (large rib)

Cooking With Shea

Shea's Osso Bucco

Preparation Time
15 minutes

Cooking Time
240 minutes

Ingredients (serves 4)

- 1/4 cup (60ml) olive oil
- 2 brown onions, chopped
- 2 carrots, chopped
- 1/2 celery stick, chopped
- Salt & freshly ground pepper
- 1.5kg veal osso bucco
- Bacon
- 1 cup (250ml) red wine
- 2 x 440g can peeled tomatoes
- 4 garlic cloves, crushed
- Ginger
- Basil
- Chopped fresh parsley
- Chopped fresh thyme
- Chopped fresh marjoram
- Chopped fresh chives
- Anchovies
- Lemon Rind
- Creamy mashed potato, to serve

Marinade

Marinade Osso Bucco shanks in a Tupperware Container and refrigerate for hours if possible. Put Osso Bucco in container and cover with Red Wine, adding on top (Pepper and Salt, Red Wine, Thyme, Marjoram, Chives, Parsley, Ginger, Basil, Garlic, Bacon, Lemon Rind, Onion, Peeled Tomatoes, Anchovies).

Method

Preheat oven to 160°C. After marinading meat, place meat and marinade in an oiled deep oven proof casserole dish. Make sure that meat is covered with enough liquid over the top of the meat. Cover the casserole dish securely with lid and cook for 2 ½ hours then place in dish chopped celery and carrots and cook for a further 1 ½ hours or until meat is very tender and the sauce thickens. Sprinkle with Parsley and Serve with Potato Mash.

Martina's Farmhouse Casserole

1 ½ kg Gravy Beef (cubed)

30 grams Butter

1-2 Carrots chopped

1-2 Onions chopped

2 sticks Celery chopped

1 Clove of Garlic (crushed)

Plain Flour

30 grams Butter Extra

2 tbspns Oil

425 gram Can Peeled Tomatoes

¼ cup Dry Red Wine or Beef Stock

1 Cup of Water

1 small Beef Stock cube Crumbled

1 tspn Grated Lemon Rind

¼ Cup Lemon Juice

Method

Heat butter in a pan, add carrot, onion, celery and garlic, stir over heat for about 5 to 10 minutes, transfer to a 10 Cup capacity casserole dish. Toss beef in plain flour, shake away excess flour.

Heat extra butter and oil in the same pan, add beef cook until well browned all over.

Place beef over vegetable mixture. Combine undrained, crushed tomatoes, wine, water, stock cube, rind and juice in same pan, bring to boil.

Pour mixture over beef, cover and cook in moderate oven for about 3 hours or until meat is tender.   Serves 4. Suitable to freeze but not to microwave.

Martina's Notes: When I make it I don't use garlic, wine or lemon rind or juice. It tastes great without those ingredients.

Cooking With Shea

1 ½ kg Gravy Beef (cubed)	2 tbspns Oil
30 grams Butter	425 gram Can Peeled Tomatoes
1-2 Carrots chopped	¼ cup Dry Red Wine or Beef Stock
1-2 Onions chopped	1 Cup of Water
2 sticks Celery chopped	1 small Beef Stock cube Crumbled
1 Clove of Garlic (crushed)	1 tspn Grated Lemon Rind
Plain Flour	¼ Cup Lemon Juice
30 grams Butter Extra	

Heat butter in a pan, add carrot, onion, celery and garlic, stir over heat for about 5 to 10 minutes, transfer to a 10 Cup capacity casserole dish. Toss beef in plain flour, shake away excess flour.

Heat extra butter and oil in the same pan, add beef cook until well browned all over.

Place beef over vegetable mixture. Combine undrained, crushed tomatoes, wine, water, stock cube, rind and juice in same pan, bring to boil.

Pour mixture over beef, cover and cook in moderate oven for about 3 hours or until meat is tender.

Serves 4. Suitable to freeze but not to microwave.

Martina's Notes: When I make it I don't use garlic, wine or lemon rind or juice. It tastes great without those ingredients.

Cooking With Shea

"Martina's" Corned Beef

Corned Beef Piece
¼ Cup Brown Vinegar
2 Onions Quartered
Water Just Covering Corned Beef Piece

Bring to the Boil

Then simmer for 2 Hours
Stab meat to check if there is not blood existing the Corned Beef Piece

Woolworths Corned Beef Recipe

1.5 Kilo Corned Beef Piece

Place Meat in a large Saucepan cover with Cold Water

Bring to Boil and simmer.

Allow approximately 60 minutes cooking time

Per kilogram or until cooked thoroughly.

Add 1 cup of vinegar, 1 tablespoon of brown sugar, some cloves and nutmeg to the water and cook as per above instructions.

Serve hot with parsley sauce and roast potatoes.

Cooking With Shea

Martina's Corn Meat

When cooked take out put onto a plate, let it cool then cover with Cling Wrap.

Put Cornbeef into a Large Pot, cover with water, add

2 Onions Quartered

2 Large Carrots Sliced

¼ cup Brown Vinegar

Then put the lid on.

Bring to the boil, for roughly 1 hour

Then simmer until cooked or tender.

Stab with a sharp knife or fork and if

No red juices come out it is cooked.

Happy Cooking.

Glazed Corned Beef

I simply love a good corned beef dinner, I have been making this particular recipe for at least 20 years now. I cook this corned beef every St. Patrick's day, the whole family just loves it. It takes a little work to prepare it but not so much that you can't still do other things around the house. This is the best tasting corned beef I have ever had in my life, it is so moist, tender, juicy and flavorful. So many recipes are still moist and tender but also flavorless.

Ingredients

4-5 Lbs. - Corned Beef (with pickling packet)
2 - Bottles Beer (your favorite brand)
1 - Lemon (large)
1 - Orange (large)
1 - Large Onion (quartered)
Water to Cover

The Glaze

1 C. - Brown Sugar
1 Tbs. - Dijon Mustard
1 C. - Apple Juice
1 C. - Orange Juice
4 Tbs. - Lemon Juice

Place the meat into a large soup pot, add the beer and enough water to cover the meat. Add the onion and pickling packet to the pot , cut the fruit and squeeze the juice into the water then place the fruit halves into the water also. Cover and simmer over medium low heat for 4 hours, when done take the lid off and let the meat cool off in the cooking liquid, about 1 hour. Take the meat out of the cooking liquid and place into a baking dish, top the meat with the brown sugar. In a bowl mix the remaining ingredients and pour around the meat. Bake in a 350 degree oven for 1 hour basting every 10-15 minutes.

WHITE SAUCE
MICROWAVE

2 tablespoons butter

2 tablesppons plain flour

Salt and pepper

300mls milk

1. Place butter into a microwave proof bowl
2. Microwave on HIGH for 40 seconds
3. Add flour, salt and pepper,
4. Stir Well
5. Cook for a further 30 seconds on HIGH
6. Gradually add milk. It is important to slowly add milk to prevent lumps forming. Microwave on HIGH for 2 minutes, stir and cook a further 2 ½ minutes on HIGH
7. Beat Sauce Well

Add 2 tablespoons freshly chopped parsley at the end of this stage. Unless leave plain.

Cooking With Shea

Shea's Corned Beef Silverside

1.5kg Piece of Silverside

1 Cup Brown Vinegar

1 Large Tablespoon Brown Sugar

Cloves

Garlic

Water

Carrots, Celery, Parsley, Pepper, Honey, Mushrooms, Cauliflower, Peas.

Marinade Silverside Overnight in Tupperware Container with Red Wine, Port, Honey, Garlic Marinade.

Put Silverside into Large Boiling Pot

Add Marinade, Cloves, Parsley, Pepper and More Honey, Carrots, Celery, Mushrooms, Cauliflower, Peas, Water to Cover Silverside.

Bring to the Boil then Simmer for Two Hours.

BBQ RIBS

Preheat Oven to 150°c

Put Ribs into Pyrex Dish

Rub with Mediterranean Seasonings

Cover with Alfoil cook for 1 hour

Take off Alfoil and cook for

A further 30 minutes.

Rest for 10 minutes

American Spare Ribs

Preheat Fan Forced Oven

150°Celsius

Cover Ribs with Alfoil

Cook for 1 hour covered

Remove Alfoil

Cook uncovered at 180°Celsius

Cook for 30 minutes

Rest for 10 Minutes

Cooking With Shea

QUICK CONVERSION GUIDE

Wherever you live in the world you can use our recipes with the help of our easy-to-follow conversions for all your cooking needs. These conversions are approximate only. The difference between the exact and approximate conversions of liquid and dry measures amounts to only a teaspoon or two, and will not make any difference to your cooking results.

MEASURING EQUIPMENT

The difference between measuring cups internationally is minimal within 2 or 3 teaspoons' difference. (For the record, 1 Australian metric measuring cup will hold approximately 250ml.) The most accurate way of measuring dry ingredients is to weigh them. When measuring liquids use a clear glass or plastic jug with metric markings.

If you would like the measuring cups and spoons as used in our Test Kitchen, turn to page 128 for details and order coupon. In this book we use metric measuring cups and spoons approved by Standards Australia.

- a graduated set of four cups for measuring dry ingredients; the sizes are marked on the cups.
- a graduated set of four spoons for measuring dry and liquid ingredients; the amounts are marked on the spoons.
- 1 TEASPOON: 5ml.
- 1 TABLESPOON: 20ml.

**NOTE: NZ, CANADA, USA AND UK ALL USE 15ml TABLESPOONS.
ALL CUP AND SPOON MEASUREMENTS ARE LEVEL.**

DRY MEASURES

METRIC	IMPERIAL
15g	½oz
30g	1oz
60g	2oz
90g	3oz
125g	4oz (¼lb)
155g	5oz
185g	6oz
220g	7oz
250g	8oz (½lb)
280g	9oz
315g	10oz
345g	11oz
375g	12oz (¾lb)
410g	13oz
440g	14oz
470g	15oz
500g	16oz (1lb)
750g	24oz (1½lb)
1kg	32oz (2lb)

LIQUID MEASURES

METRIC	IMPERIAL
30ml	1 fluid oz
60ml	2 fluid oz
100ml	3 fluid oz
125ml	4 fluid oz
150ml	5 fluid oz (¼ pint/1 gill)
190ml	6 fluid oz
250ml	8 fluid oz
300ml	10 fluid oz (½ pint)
500ml	16 fluid oz
600ml	20 fluid oz (1 pint)
1000ml (1 litre)	1¾ pints

WE USE LARGE EGGS WITH AN AVERAGE WEIGHT OF 60g

HELPFUL MEASURES

METRIC	IMPERIAL
3mm	⅛in
6mm	¼in
1cm	½in
2cm	¾in
2.5cm	1in
5cm	2in
6cm	2½in
8cm	3in
10cm	4in
13cm	5in
15cm	6in
18cm	7in
20cm	8in
23cm	9in
25cm	10in
28cm	11in
30cm	12in (1ft)

HOW TO MEASURE

When using the graduated metric measuring cups, it is important to shake the dry ingredients loosely into the required cup. Do not tap the cup on the bench, or pack the ingredients into the cup unless otherwise directed. Level top of cup with knife. When using graduated metric measuring spoons, level top of spoon with knife. When measuring liquids in the jug, place jug on flat surface, check for accuracy at eye level.

OVEN TEMPERATURES

These oven temperatures are only a guide; we've given you the lower degree of heat. Always check the manufacturer's manual.

	C° (Celsius)	F° (Fahrenheit)	Gas Mark
Very slow	120	250	1
Slow	150	300	2
Moderately slow	160	325	3
Moderate	180 – 190	350 – 375	4
Moderately hot	200 – 210	400 – 425	5
Hot	220 – 230	450 – 475	6
Very hot	240 – 250	500 – 525	7

Cooking With Shea

Marco's Perfect Steak

Olive Oil

Rosemary

Salt

Lemon Juice

Beef (Eye of Meat) Sirloin Steak

Fat On Meat

Oil Grill or Grid

Olive Oil on Steak

Oil Grid

Season Meat with Salt

Cook for 5 minutes on Hot Gridle

Turn after Five Minutes

Put Rosemary on Cooked Side of Meat

Turn Off Heat

Put Lemon Juice on Steak

HOMESTEAD MEATLOAF

- **Ingredients**

  - 350g thinly sliced pancetta*
  - 2 teaspoons olive oil
  - 1 onion, finely chopped
  - 3 garlic cloves, finely chopped
  - 750g beef mince
  - 1 tablespoon brandy
  - 5 dried juniper berries*, finely crushed
  - 1/4 teaspoon mixed spice
  - 60g toasted pine nuts, roughly chopped
  - 1/2 cup finely chopped flat-leaf parsley

Cooking With Shea

1. Step 1

    Preheat oven to 190°C. Grease and line a 1-litre loaf pan, leaving enough overhanging to cover the top. Set aside 16 pancetta slices and finely chop the rest (about 200g).

2. Step 2

    Heat oil in a frypan over low heat. Fry onion and garlic for 3-4 minutes or until soft, then cool. Use your hands to combine mince, onion mixture, chopped pancetta, brandy, juniper, spice, nuts, parsley, salt and pepper.

3. Step 3

    Line pan with reserved pancetta slices, slightly overlapping and extending over edges. Spoon mixture into pan, press down firmly, then top with remaining pancetta. Fold in edges and paper to enclose. Cover with foil and bake for 50 minutes. Remove foil and stand for 15 minutes. Drain juices and invert meatloaf onto a board. Serve 2-3cm slices, warm or cold, with chutney and spinach.

Cooking With Shea

Healthy meatloaf

- **Ingredients**

  - ☐ 500g extra lean beef mince
  - ☐ 1 cup fresh wholemeal breadcrumbs
  - ☐ 1 small brown onion, grated
  - ☐ 1 carrot, peeled, coarsely grated
  - ☐ 2 tablespoons tomato sauce
  - ☐ 2 tablespoons flat-leaf parsley leaves, chopped
  - ☐ 1 egg, lightly beaten
  - ☐ 1/4 cup barbecue sauce
  - ☐ 8 chat potatoes, halved
  - ☐ 1 bunch Dutch carrots, peeled, trimmed
  - ☐ 150g green beans, trimmed

Cooking With Shea

Preheat oven to 180°C. Line a baking tray with baking paper. Place mince, breadcrumbs, onion, carrot, tomato sauce, parsley and egg in a large bowl. Season with salt and pepper. Using clean hands, mix until well combined.

1. Step 2

   Shape mince into a 10cm x 18cm rectangle. Place on prepared tray. Bake for 25 to 30 minutes or until firm to touch. Remove from oven. Drain excess fat.

2. Step 3

   Spoon barbecue sauce over top of meatloaf. Return to oven and cook for a further 10 minutes or until top is glazed. Stand on tray for 5 minutes.

3. Step 4

   Meanwhile, place potato, carrot and beans in separate microwave-safe plastic bags. Twist tops to seal. Microwave each on HIGH (100%) for 1 1/2 to 2 minutes or until almost tender. Slice meatloaf. Serve with vegetables.

Cooking With Shea

Shea's Classic Meatloaf

• Ingredients

- ☐ 1 tablespoon olive oil
- ☐ 1 brown onion, finely chopped
- ☐ 2 garlic cloves, crushed
- ☐ 1 1/2 cups fresh breadcrumbs or chopped up fresh bread
- ☐ 500g beef mince
- ☐ 300g pork and veal mince
- ☐ 1 egg, lightly beaten
- ☐ 1 tablespoon wholegrain mustard
- ☐ 2 teaspoons Worcestershire sauce
- ☐ 3/4 cup tomato sauce
- ☐ 2 tablespoons brown sugar
- ☐ 2 tablespoons oregano – finely chopped
- ☐ 2 tablespoons parsley – finely chopped

- **You can use more oregano and more parsley if you wish**
- **You can use 3 eggs to make it more moist if you wish**
- **You can use 2 cups of bread if you wish**

- ☐ Mashed potato, steamed green beans and gravy or any vegetables

Cooking With Shea

1. Step 1

   Preheat oven to 200°C/180°C fan-forced. Grease a 9cm-deep, 9cm x 19cm (base) loaf pan with butter. Heat oil in a medium frying pan over medium heat. Add onion and garlic. Cook, stirring, for 5 minutes or until onion has softened. Set aside for 5 minutes to cool down in temperature.

2. Step 2

   Place onion, breadcrumbs, minces, egg, mustard, Worcestershire sauce and 1/2 cup tomato sauce in a bowl. Mix to combine. Spoon into pan. Level top with a spoon.

3. Step 3

   Combine sugar and remaining sauce in a small bowl. Spread over top of mince. Bake for 1 hour or until meatloaf is browned and comes away from sides of pan. Drain juices from pan. Set aside for 5 minutes. Serve with potato, green beans and gravy.

Classic meatloaf

- **Ingredients**

  - ☐ 1 tablespoon olive oil
  - ☐ 1 brown onion, finely chopped
  - ☐ 2 garlic cloves, crushed
  - ☐ 1 1/2 cups fresh breadcrumbs
  - ☐ 500g beef mince
  - ☐ 300g pork and veal mince
  - ☐ 1 egg, lightly beaten
  - ☐ 1 tablespoon wholegrain mustard
  - ☐ 2 teaspoons Worcestershire sauce
  - ☐ 3/4 cup tomato sauce
  - ☐ 2 tablespoons brown sugar
  - ☐ Mashed potato, steamed green beans and gravy, to serve
    - ☐ Oregano, finely chopped
    - ☐ Parsely, finely chopped

1. Step 1

    Preheat oven to 200°C/180°C fan-forced. Grease a 9cm-deep, 9cm x 19cm (base) loaf pan. Heat oil in a medium frying pan over medium heat. Add onion and garlic. Cook, stirring, for 5 minutes or until onion has softened. Set aside for 5 minutes to cool.

2. Step 2

    Place onion, breadcrumbs, minces, egg, mustard, Worcestershire sauce and 1/2 cup tomato sauce in a bowl. Mix to combine. Spoon into pan. Level top with a spoon.

3. Step 3

    Combine sugar and remaining sauce in a small bowl. Spread over top of mince. Bake for 1 hour or until meatloaf is browned and comes away from sides of pan. Drain juices from pan. Set aside for 5 minutes. Serve with potato, green beans and gravy.

Cakes and Sweets Recipes

SHEA'S ROCKY ROAD

INGREDIENTS

200g Dark Chocolate
200g Milk Chocolate
40g Unsalted Butter
150g Marshmallows
150g Glace Cherries
120g Blanched Almonds
75g Cranberries
100g Apricot Indulgence Pieces

METHOD

Melt Chocolate in Pot over Pot of Simmering Water
Do not allow the Chocolate Pot to touch the Simmering Water.
Put all the Ingredients into a large bowl and stir in melted chocolate.
Put mixture into a tray lined with Baking Paper.
Then refrigerate for at least two hours.

Cooking With Shea

Ingredients

4 oz	butter or margarine
1 tbls	golden syrup
2 tbls	boiling water
1 ½ tsp	bicarbonate of soda
1 cup	rolled oats
¾ cup	desiccated coconut
1 cup (4 oz)	plain flour
1 cup (8 oz)	sugar

Method

Melt butter and golden syrup over gentle heat, add mixed boiling water and bicarbonate of soda. Pour into mixed dry ingredients, blend well. Drop teaspoonfuls of mixture on greased tray.
Bake in slow oven (300°F) for 20 minutes. Cool on trays a few minutes, remove and store in airtight containers when cool. Makes about 4 dozen.

SHEA'S ORANGE DATE MUFFINS

1	**Whole Orange**
1	**Egg**
½ cup	**Orange Juice**
½ cup	**Chopped Dates**
½ cup	**Butter (4 ozs)**
1 ½ cups	**Plain Flour**
1 tsp.	**Baking Soda**
1 tsp.	**Baking Powder**

Cut the Orange into pieces to remove seeds.
Blend these pieces with ½ cup Orange Juice until all is finely chopped.
Drop in the dates, egg and butter and give a short whiz.
Pour orange mixture over dry ingredients and stir lightly just until moistened.

Scoop into muffin trays or patty skins.

Bake in Oven (375 degrees) for around (15 to 20 mins).

Sultanas can be used rather than dates.

Cooking With Shea

Jo Woulfe's

BANANA CAKE

INGREDIENTS

125GRAMS	BUTTER or MARGARINE
1 CUP	BROWN SUGAR
2	EGGS
3	RIPE BANANAS
1 TEASPOON	CARB. SODA
1 TABLESPOON	MILK
1 ½ CUPS	SELF RAISING FLOUR
SOME	VANILLA

Cream Butter and Sugar, Add Eggs, Mashed Bananas, Vanilla and Carb. Soda mixed with Milk, last add Flour.

Bake about 45 minutes in a Moderate Oven. **180° to 190°**

Cooking With Shea

Chris' Banana Bread

INGREDIENTS

- 1 1/2 cups (225g) plain flour
- 1 tsp baking powder
- 1 tsp salt
- 1 tsp ground cinnamon
- 1/2 cup (110g) caster sugar
- 1 egg
- 1/3 cup (80ml) sunflower oil
- 1 tsp vanilla extract
- 4 ripe bananas, mashed
- 65g pecan nuts, roughly chopped
- Butter and honey, to serve

1. **Preheat** the **oven** to **180°C**. Grease and line the base of a 900ml loaf pan.
2. Sift the flour, baking powder, cinnamon and sugar with 1 teaspoon of salt into a large bowl. In a separate bowl, combine the egg, oil and vanilla.
3. Add to the dry ingredients with banana and pecan and fold until just combined - do not overmix.
4. Place into the loaf pan and **bake for 50 minutes** or until golden. Allow to cool for 10 minutes, then remove, and slice thickly. Serve spread with butter and drizzled with honey.

CHERRY CRUMBLE RECIPE

2 x 415g Stoneless Black Cherries in Syrup drained
Reserve ¼ cup of Syrup
½ cup of Almond Meal
¼ cup of Plain Flour
¼ cup of Brown Sugar
½ cup of Shredded Coconut
¼ tspn of Nutmeg
70g Butter cubed

Preheat oven to 200c. Grease a three cup (750ml) oven proof dish. Place cherries in the prepared dish and pour the reserved juice on top.
Combine the Almond Meal, Flour, Sugar, Coconut and Nutmeg in a bowl.
Rub butter into the mixture and spread it across the top of the cherries.
Bake for 15 minutes or until the crumb is golden.
Serve with cream or ice cream.

Serves 4
Prep time 10 mins
Cooking time 15 minutes

Fudgy Chocolate Cake

A decadent chocolate layer cake covered with rich, delicious chocolate icing – an all-time favourite that's moist to the very last crumb!

Cooking With Shea

Ingredients
SERVES 8

- 190g/6oz white chocolate, for garnish
- 250g/8oz unsalted butter
- 1 cup plus 3 tbsp caster sugar
- 1½ cups plain flour
- ½ cup plus 3 tbsp unsweetened cocoa powder
- 1 tbsp baking powder
- 1 tsp salt
- 4 large eggs
- 250ml/8fl oz cream
- 315g/10½ oz plain chocolate

SERVING SUGGESTION

Who doesn't love cake and ice-cream? Serve this rich cake with your favourite ice-cream flavour.

Nutritional information per serving: kilojoules 3129/calories 745, fat 48.4g (sat fat 28.1g), carbs 76.5g

Easy Step-by-Step

1. Finely grate the white chocolate using a vegetable peeler. Chill until needed. Preheat oven to 180°C/350°F.

2. Grease the base of two 20cm/8in round cake pans; line with baking paper. Combine butter, sugar, flour, cocoa, baking powder, salt and eggs in a large bowl. Using an electric mixer set on medium, beat until smooth. Continue beating until increased in volume, about 2 minutes longer. Divide batter between pans.

3. Bake cakes until a toothpick inserted in centres comes out clean, 20–25 minutes. Leave cakes in pans to cool for 1 minute, then turn onto a wire rack. Peel off lining paper; let cool.

4. Meanwhile, heat cream just to the boil. Break chocolate into pieces; add to cream and stir until melted. Let cool; chill for 30 minutes, then whisk until thickened to a spreadable consistency.

5. Use a third of chocolate icing to sandwich cakes. Spread the remainder over the whole cake. Sprinkle reserved grated white chocolate over.

Great Ideas

For a super-light cake, be sure to beat the cake mixture thoroughly to introduce plenty of air into it, encouraging the cake to rise.

Rosemary, Feta and Walnut Damper

3 cups self-raising flour
1/4 cup Rosemary sprigs
2 tbls Moroccan seasoning
2 tbls salt
80 grams cold butter, chopped
100 grams Feta cheese
1/3 cup walnuts
3/4 cup of milk

1 - Preheat oven to 200C
2 - Sift flour and add Rosemary seasoning, salt and combine
3 - Rub butter into the above mixture until it resembles fine breadcrumbs
4 - Stir Feta and walnuts into the mixture
5 - Combine 1/2 cup of milk with 1/2 cup of water
6 - Stir with cold knife until the mixture comes together
7 - Turn on lightly floured surface
8 - Cut into appropriate pieces - cut on top in cross
9 - Dash lightly with remaining milk
10 - Bake 25 minutes or until brown

Triple Treat Biscuits — Makes about 48

BASIC BISCUIT DOUGH:
250g butter or dairy blend, chopped
1 teaspoons vanilla essence OR few drops almond essence
1/2 cup castor sugar
2 cups plain flour

desiccated coconut
halved glace cherries
cocoa powder
chocolate buttons
beaten egg white
additional castor sugar
unblanched almonds

Place butter, castor sugar and essence into a food processor and blend together. Add flour gradually until a soft dough is formed.

Remove 2/3 of the dough from the processor. Roll half this mixture into small balls, then coat with the coconut and press a half cherry on top.

Roll the remaining dough into rounds, then into beaten egg white and a little castor sugar. Top each with an almond.

Add to the remainder of the dough in the processor 1 tablespoon of cocoa and work in. Shape mixture into small balls, press a chocolate button into each.

Arrange biscuits on Willow Large Biscuit Tray and bake in a preheated 180°C oven for 12 - 15 minutes.

CHICKEN RECIPES

Cooking with Shea

Shea's Roast Chicken

No: 23 Chicken or 2.3 Kilos

180°C Fan Forced Oven

22 minutes per 500 grams

2 kilos = 88 minutes
0.3 kilos = 13 minutes

Total Cooking Time for No: 23 Chicken

101 minutes
Or
1 hour 41 minutes

No: 20 Chicken or 2.0 kilos

180°C Fan Forced Oven

22 minutes per 500 grams

2 kilos = 88 minutes

Seasoning

Stuffing Mix, 2 Eggs, Lemon Thyme, Sage, Sultanas, Pepper, Cumin

Chicken Maryland

4 Chicken Marylands
Brandy
Chicken Stock Cube
Water
Tarragon
Honey
Pepper

Place 4 Chicken Marylands in a Pyrex Oven Dish.
Pour in some Water and a Chicken Stock Cube
Pour Brandy over Chicken
Sprinkle Tarragon over Chicken
Sprinkle Pepper over Chicken
Pour Honey over Chicken

Place in the Preheated Fan Forced Oven at 200° Celsius

Cook for 1 hour

Cooking with Shea

Shea's Braised Chicken Legs

Ingredients

Chicken Legs

Red Wine

Garlic Cloves Sliced

Thyme

Parsley

Sage

Lemon Zest

Yoghurt

Honey

Orange Slices

Chicken Stock

Brandy

Cooking with Shea

Marinade Chicken Legs over night in Red Wine, Herbs, Brandy, Garlic Cloves.

Oil Deep Casserole Dish. Place Orange Slices on the bottom of dish.

Place Chicken Legs on top of Orange Slices.

Add (1 ½) cups of Red Wine then (½) cup of Chicken Stock. Add (4) Garlic Cloves sliced then drizzle Honey over legs then add some Herbs, then pour (1 kg) of Yoghurt over legs then sprinkle Lemon Zest plus more herbs, then grind Pepper on top.

Then put the Lid on top of Casserole Dish.

Bake in oven at (150· c) for (3 ½) hours.

CHICKEN MARENGO

Chicken Marengo - *named for being the dish that Napoleon ate after the Battle of Marengo and his chef was forced to work with the meager results of a forage.*

Ingredients
5 boneless, skinless chicken breasts, cut into pieces
2 tablespoons olive oil
2 medium onions, chopped
1 tablespoon flour
1/2 cup water
1/4 cup dry white wine
3 tablespoons tomato paste
1 clove garlic, crushed
1/4 teaspoon thyme
1 bay leaf
1/2 teaspoon salt
1/4 teaspoon black pepper
1/2 pound mushrooms, chopped
1 tablespoon chopped parsley

Heat oil in a large nonstick skillet over medium heat until hot. Add chicken and quickly brown on all sides. Add onions and cook until onions are slightly browned. Sprinkle with flour and cook for 3 minutes stirring constantly. Add the water, wine, tomato paste, garlic, thyme, bay leaf, salt and pepper and bring to a boil. Reduce heat, cover and simmer gently for 30 minutes or until chicken is tender and no longer pink. Remove chicken to serving dish and keep warm. Add mushrooms to skillet and cover and cook over low heat for 15 minutes. Pour mushroom mixture over chicken and sprinkle with parsley. Can be served over rice or pasta.

Chicken Marengo Recipe

5 boneless, skinless chicken breasts, cut into pieces
2 tablespoons olive oil
2 medium onions, chopped
1 tablespoon flour
1/2 cup water
1/4 cup dry white wine
3 tablespoons tomato paste
1 clove garlic, crushed
1/4 teaspoon thyme
1 bay leaf
1/2 teaspoon salt
1/4 teaspoon black pepper
1/2 pound mushrooms, chopped
1 tablespoon chopped parsley

Heat oil in a large nonstick skillet over medium heat until hot. Add chicken and quickly brown on all sides. Add onions and cook until onions are slightly browned. Sprinkle with flour and cook for 3 minutes stirring constantly. Add the water, wine, tomato paste, garlic, thyme, bay leaf, salt and pepper and bring to a boil. Reduce heat, cover and simmer gently for 30 minutes or until chicken is tender and no longer pink. Remove chicken to serving dish and keep warm. Add mushrooms to skillet and cover and cook over low heat for 15 minutes. Pour mushroom mixture over chicken and sprinkle with parsley. Can be served over rice or pasta.

Makes 6 Servings

Cooking with Shea

Chicken Cutlets – Oven Baked

INGREDIENTS

Two Chicken Cutlets Per Person

Two Onions

Port

Two Small Potatoes Per Person

Carrots

Broccoli

Asparagus

Squash

Kumara

Butternut Pumpkin

Cooking with Shea

Marinate Chicken Cutlets in Port Overnight

Put Chicken Cutlets and Port and Chopped Onion in Pyrex Baking Tray

Julienne Carrots

Peel and Slice Kumara

Slice Butternut Pumpkin into small pieces

Slice Broccoli into lengths

Cut Asparagus into lengths

Small Potatoes

Preheat Oven to 180° Degrees

Cooking Time One Hour

Put Chicken Cutlets in Pyrex Tray into Pre Heated Oven on Bottom Shelf

Put Small Potatoes on the Top Shelf by themselves same time as Chicken Cutlets

On a flat oiled tray put on Sliced Pumpkin and Sliced Kumara on Top Shelf

Cook all of these ingredients for one hour

Put Squash into Saucepan with Boiling Water – Cook for 20 minutes

Put Carrots into Saucepan with Boiling Water Cook for 15 minutes

Put Broccoli into Saucepan with Steamer with Boiling Water Cook for 5 minutes

Put Asparagus into Saucepan with Boiling Water Cook for 2 minutes

ROAST CHICKEN WITH COUSCOUS

SERVES 4

INGREDIENTS

- 1 x 1.6kg whole macro free-range chicken
- 1 lemon
- olive oil
- sea salt and freshly ground black pepper
- 1 heaped teaspoon ground cumin
- 2 red onions
- 2 carrots
- 200g jarred roasted red peppers
- 1 teaspoon smoked paprika
- 1 tablespoon ground coriander
- 250g couscous
- a few sprigs of fresh mint
- extra virgin olive oil

JAMIE'S TIP

Basting a chicken as it cooks helps to stop it drying out, giving you lovely, juicy meat. Check on the chicken every 20 to 30 minutes, and spoon any juices from the bottom of the tray back over the bird.

METHOD

1. Preheat the oven to 200°C. Place the chicken on a board and make some deep crisscross slashes into the legs – this will help the spices to penetrate the meat, and will also help it to cook more quickly. Halve the lemon and place inside the chicken, then rub the chicken skin all over with olive oil, a little sea salt, pepper and the cumin. Transfer the chicken to a roasting tray and place in the hot oven.

2. Peel and quarter the onions and carrots. When the chicken's been cooking for around 15 minutes, reduce the heat to 180°C and add the onions and carrots to the tray. Roast for a further hour, or until golden and cooked through – the chicken is cooked when the thigh meat pulls easily away from the bone and the juices run clear.

3. Once perfectly cooked, carefully lift the chicken onto a plate or board and cover with tin foil and a couple of tea towels to keep warm. Spoon the vegetables onto a board and roughly chop them, then tip back into the tray and place on a medium heat. Pour in 500ml boiling water and stir well, making sure you scrape up all the lovely sticky goodness from the bottom of the tray.

4. Drain and roughly chop the peppers, then add them to the tray with the smoked paprika, ground coriander and the couscous. Pull the lemon halves out of the chicken with a pair of tongs and squeeze the juices into the tray (making sure to catch any pips). Bring to the boil, then turn the heat off and leave to rest for 5 minutes, or until the couscous has absorbed all of the water. Meanwhile, pick and finely chop the mint leaves. When the time's up, fluff up the couscous using a fork and stir through the chopped mint. Drizzle with a good lug of extra virgin olive oil and everything together.

5. Cut the chicken up into joints, removing the skin if you want to keep it healthy, then serve with the tasty roast-vegetable couscous. Enjoy!

Chicken Thigh Cutlets Cooked in a Baccarat Dutch Oven

SHEA'S INGREDIENTS

4 Large Chicken Thigh Cutlets

Port + Red Wine + Raisins + Morello Cherries in a Jar

Sage + Pepper + Garlic

Extra Virgin Olive Oil

Marinade Cutlets overnight in Port and Red Wine and Morello Cherries and Raisins enough liquid to almost cover Chicken Thigh Cutlets in Tupperware Container

Preheat Oven/Stove to 180°celsius

Put oil in the bottom of the Dutch Oven then put Chicken Thigh Cutlets in Dutch Oven then pour over Port and Red Wine and Morello Cherry and Raisins Liquid combination almost covering Chicken Thigh Cutlets

Spread Ground Sage, Ground Pepper, Minced Garlic over Top of Chicken

Put Lid on Top of Dutch Oven and cook for 50 minutes in your Oven/Stove.

Remove from Dutch Oven and serve and enjoy with vegetables

Chicken Thighs

Oven Baked in a Dutch Oven 6.3 litre

INGREDIENTS

6 Large Chicken Thigh Cutlets
Marinade of Port/Red Wine/Lemon Thyme/Pepper/Minced Garlic
Oil
2 Onions
1 Can Tinned Tomatoes
Oregano
Honey
Brown Sugar
4 Apples Cut Into Thin Slices

Marinade Chicken/Port/Red Wine/Lemon Thyme/Pepper/Minced Garlic
In a Tupperware Container overnight covering chicken totally with liquid

Put oil in Dutch Oven spreading oil all over the inside of Dutch Oven
Then slice onions and oregano and apples and put into Dutch Oven
Put marinated Chicken and Liquid into the Dutch Oven
Then spread Brown Sugar and Honey over the Chicken Thigh Cutlets
Put tinned tomatoes over the Chicken Thigh Cutlets
Make sure liquid covers Chicken Thigh Cutlets totally.

Preheat Fan Forced Oven to 160°c
Put Lid on Dutch Oven and place into 160°c oven
Cook Chicken for 60 minutes = 1 hour

4 CHICKEN & POULTRY

Lemon Grilled Chicken

Tasty herbs complete a mouthwatering marinade that flavours golden chicken breasts – just grill and enjoy. Perfect for family feasts and barbecues!

Cooking with Shea

Lemon Grilled Chicken

Prep Time **40 mins**   Cook Time **20 mins**

Ingredients
SERVES 4

- 1 lemon
- 2 tbsp olive oil
- 1 clove garlic, crushed
- 1 tbsp chopped fresh parsley, plus extra sprigs for garnish
- ¼ tsp dried thyme
- ¼ tsp dried marjoram
- ¼ tsp salt
- ¼ tsp black pepper
- 4 chicken breast fillets (about 190g/6oz each)

SERVING SUGGESTION

For a healthy meal, serve with grilled button mushrooms and a pasta salad mixed with zucchini and capsicums.

Nutritional information per serving:
kilojoules 1058/calories 252, fat 8.9g (sat fat 1.5g), carbs 1.7g

Easy Step-by-Step

1. Use a peeler to remove strips of zest from half the lemon, then trim into fine strips with a small knife. Reserve and set aside. Grate the other side of the lemon to make 1 tablespoon zest. Finally, squeeze the juice from the lemon into a bowl.

2. In a large bowl, combine zest and juice, oil, garlic, parsley, thyme, marjoram, salt and pepper. Add the chicken to the bowl and spoon the marinade over until well coated. Cover with plastic wrap. Chill for 30 minutes, or overnight if you have time.

3. Preheat a ridged griddle pan to medium. Put the chicken on the griddle, reserving marinade. Cook chicken until cooked through, about 10 minutes on each side. Brush with marinade 2-3 times during cooking. Sprinkle with reserved lemon strips and serve immediately garnished with parsley sprigs.

Great Ideas

The easiest way to prevent lemon zest from sticking to a grater is to brush it off with a pastry brush. You can also use the brush to baste the chicken with the marinade in Step 3.

Cooking with Shea

INGHAM'S
Turkey Leg Roast - 1.275 kg

Cooking Instructions

Cooking times are approximate only as all appliances vary.
Place leg roast on rack in oven proof dish with 1 cup water in the dish.

Fan Forced Oven

Preheat oven to 160°c and cook for **1 hour and 40 minutes** or until cooked through, turning once.

Conventional Oven

Preheat oven to 180°c and cook for **1 hour and 40 minutes** or until cooked through, turning once.

Serving Suggestions

Serve with your favourite baked vegetables or an apple walnut salad.

Shea's Roast Duck

Size 21 Duck

Preheat Oven Temperature

Cook

120 degrees for Two Hours

Then

baste with Glaze

Then

190 degrees for One Hour

Roast duck
Cranberry hoisin, crispy skin, chilli, fresh herbs & pancakes

Cooking with Shea

Serves: Six
Cooks in: 2 hours, 20 minutes
Difficulty: Not too tricky

Ingredients

1 x 2 kilo duck, giblets reserved
1 red onion
Olive oil
Chinese 5-spice powder
1 Clementine
Garnishes
4 spring onions
4 small carrots
Half a cucumber
1 fresh red chilli
1 mixed bunch of fresh mint and coriander (30 g)
1 lime
18 Chinese pancakes
Cranberry Hoison sauce
2 cloves of garlic
5cm piece of ginger
200 g frozen cranberries
2 tablespoons low-salt soy sauce
2 Clementines

Cooking with Shea

Method

1. Get your meat out of the fridge and up to room temperature before you cook it. Preheat the oven to 180ºC/350ºF/gas 4.
2. Peel the onion, cut into wedges and place in a roasting tray with the giblets and a splash of water.
3. Rub the duck all over with 1 tablespoon of oil, 1 tablespoon of Chinese five-spice and a really good pinch of sea salt.
4. Halve the clementine and place in the cavity, then sit the duck directly on the bars of the oven, with the tray of onions and giblets underneath to catch the tasty fat.
5. Roast for 2 hours, or until the duck is crispy and cooked through, turning the onions occasionally to prevent them from catching.
6. While the duck cooks, prep the garnishes. Trim and halve the spring onions and carrots, then finely slice lengthways, scratch a fork down the cucumber, and finely slice it with the chilli. Pick the herb leaves. Cut the lime into wedges.
7. Remove the cooked duck to a platter, cover, and rest for 30 minutes. Pour all the fat from the tray into a jar, cool, and place in the fridge for tasty cooking another day.
8. Now you've got a choice: you can make a dark hoisin utilizing the bonus flavour from the tray, or you can do it separately in a pan to achieve the vibrant colour you see in the picture – both ways are super-tasty, it's purely personal preference.
9. Using the tray, remove and discard the giblets, leaving the onions behind. Place over a medium heat on the hob, peel, roughly chop and add the garlic and ginger, add 1 teaspoon of five-spice, then stir in the cranberries, picking up all the sticky goodness from the base of the tray.
10. Cook for 2 minutes, then add the soy, rice wine vinegar, honey, clementine juice and a splash of water. Simmer for 5 minutes, or until thick and glossy.
11. Pour into a blender and blitz until smooth, then taste and season to perfection.
12. If you're doing it in a pan, just follow the instructions above, adding a splash of oil to the pan before the garlic, ginger and five-spice.
13. In batches, warm the pancakes in a bamboo steamer over a pan of simmering water for just 1 to 2 minutes.

Cooking with Shea

4. Slice the duck meat, or get two forks and ravage it all off the bone. Serve everything in the middle of the table so everyone builds their own. The crispy duck skin will be an absolute treat dotted on top!

Cooking with Shea

 # Roast Duck

No: 19 Duck or 1.9 kilos

180° C

Fan Forced Oven

Cook For

(100 mins) or (1 hour 40 minutes)

No: 17 Duck or 1.7 kilos

180° C

Fan Forced Oven

Cook For

(90 mins) or (1 hour 30 minutes)

Place Orange Slices in Baking Tray
Pour in the Juice from a tin of
Woolworths Stoneless Black Cherries in Syrup
Lay Duck on a bed of Orange Slices and Syrup
Splash some Brandy over the top of Duck

Seasoning

Stuffing Mix
Tin of Woolworths Stoneless Black Cherries in Syrup
Slivered Almonds
2 Eggs
Lemon Thyme
Orange Juice
Sultanas

Sauce

Orange Juice
Orange Marmalade
Honey

BBQ Duck With Noodles

Method

1. Preheat oven to 220°C
2. Season the duck with the salt and pepper, then brush with BBQ sauce.
3. Place the duck into oven skin-side-up, then immediately reduce the heat to 170°C.
4. Cook the duck for 30 minutes - or a little less if you like your duck rare - brushing with the BBQ sauce every 5 minutes. Remove from oven and rest for 10 minutes before carving.
5. Add the noodles to a saucepan of boiling water.
6. Place a wok over high heat and, once hot, add the oil. Add the onion and garlic to the wok and stir-fry for 30 seconds, then add all the vegetables and stir-fry for 2 minutes, tossing continually.
7. Drain the noodles of excess water, then add to the wok with the sauce.
8. Toss well to combine. Place the noodle mixture on a large serving platter, serve with the sliced duck on top.

Curries

Cooking with Shea

BEEF  CURRY

Description This recipe for Beef Curry is a favourite at my brother's house. I hate to admit it but it tastes yummy. There are many different Beef Curries such as Beef Rogan Josh, Beef Madras and Beef curry. This particular Indian Beef Curry recipe is very easy to make. You can even cook it the day before and freeze it. Serve the curry with some warm naan bread to enjoy this delicious Indian Beef curry recipe.

INGREDIENTS

- About 450 gm (1 lb) boneless lamb
- 3 onions
- 4 cloves of garlic
- 2.5 cm ginger
- 3 tomatoes
- 3 tbsp Ghee (Clarified Butter)
- 2 tsp ground coriander
- 1 1/2 tsp ground cumin
- 1 tsp chilli powder
- 1 tsp Garam Masala
- 1 tsp salt
- 100 ml yoghurt, lightly beaten
- 300 ml double cream
- 225 ml water

Methods/steps

- Start off by washing & drying the meat.
- Then cut the meat into small cubes about 1 in.
- Create a fine paste from the onion, garlic and ginger by blending it in a blender.
- Boil the tomatoes in boiling water for about 10 seconds then peel and chop them.
- Heat the ghee in a large saucepan and fry the paste, stirring constantly, until golden brown.
- Add the coriander, cumin, chilli, Garam Masala and stir-fry for 1 to 2 minutes.
- Add salt to taste.
- Then add the Beef and fry for a few minutes.
- Add the yoghurt, mix well and fry for a further minute.
- Add the Double Cream, mix well and fry for a further minute.
- Add the water and when it starts to boil, lower the heat to a simmer.
- Cover and cook for about 45 minutes, stirring occasionally.
- Finally add the tomatoes, stir well to mix, cover again and cook for a further 25 - 30 minutes until the lamb is tender and the gravy slightly thickened.

For garnishing, add some freshly chopped coriander.

Madras beef curry

Ingredients (serves 4)

- 2 tablespoons ground coriander
- 1 tablespoon ground cumin
- 1 teaspoon turmeric
- 1/2 teaspoon freshly ground black pepper
- 1 teaspoon chilli powder (optional)
- 2 garlic cloves, crushed
- 2 teaspoons grated ginger
- 2 1/2 tablespoons lemon juice
- 2 tablespoons olive oil
- 1kg chuck steak, cut into 2.5cm cubes
- 2 tablespoons tomato paste
- 1 cup beef stock
- steamed basmati rice, raita and mint leaves, to serve

Method

1. Combine coriander, cumin, turmeric, pepper, chilli, garlic, ginger and lemon juice in a bowl to form a paste. Set aside.
2. Heat 1 tablespoon of oil in a large saucepan over high heat. Add half the beef. Cook, stirring, for 2 to 3 minutes, or until browned. Transfer to a bowl. Repeat with remaining oil and beef.
3. Reduce heat to medium. Add spice paste. Cook for 1 minute. Return beef to saucepan. Cook, stirring, for 1 minute, or until meat is coated with paste. Add tomato paste and stock. Bring to the boil. Reduce heat to low. Cover. Cook for 1 hour 15 minutes, or until beef is tender.
4. Remove lid. Cook, uncovered, for a further 15 minutes, or until sauce has reduced and thickened slightly. Serve with rice and raita. Top with mint leaves.

Cooking with Shea

Indian Chicken Curry

Ingredients

- 2 teaspoons olive oil
- 6 x 150g single chicken breast fillets
- 1 brown onion, cut into thin wedges
- 1/4 cup Pataks Balti curry paste
- 1 cup reduced-salt chicken stock
- 400g can diced tomatoes
- 500g kumara (orange sweet potato), peeled, cut into 2cm pieces
- 200g green beans, topped, halved
- 1 1/2 cups basmati rice, cooked, to serve

Method

1. Heat 1 teaspoon of oil in a large non-stick frying pan over medium-high heat. Add chicken. Cook for 2 to 3 minutes each side or until browned. Slice.
2. Heat remaining oil in frying pan over medium heat. Add onion. Cook, stirring, for 5 minutes. Add curry paste. Cook, stirring, for 1 minute. Add stock, tomatoes and kumara. Cover. Bring to the boil. Reduce heat to medium-low. Simmer, partially covered, for 10 minutes.
3. Add chicken to frying pan. Cover. Cook for 5 minutes. Add beans. Cook, covered, for a further 5 minutes or until chicken is cooked through. Serve with rice.

Cooking with Shea

SHEA'S LAMB CURRY

Description This recipe for Lamb Curry is a favourite at my brother's house. I hate to admit it but it tastes yummy. There are many different Lamb Curries such as Lamb Rogan Josh, Lamb Madras and Lamb curry. This particular Indian Lamb Curry recipe is very easy to make. You can even cook it the day before and freeze it. Serve the curry with some warm naan bread to enjoy this delicious Indian lamb curry recipe.

INGREDIENTS

- About 450 gm (1 lb) boneless lamb
- 3 onions
- 4 cloves of garlic
- 2.5 cm ginger
- 3 tomatoes
- 3 tbsp Ghee (Clarified Butter)
- 2 tsp ground coriander
- 1 1/2 tsp ground cumin
- 1 tsp chilli powder
- 1 tsp Garam Masala
- 1 tsp salt
- 200 ml yoghurt, lightly beaten
- 200 ml double cream
- 225 ml water

Method

- Start off by washing & drying the meat.
- Then cut the meat into small cubes about 1 in.
- Create a fine paste from the onion, garlic and ginger by blending it in a blender.
- Boil the tomatoes in boiling water for about 10 seconds then peel and chop them.
- Heat the ghee in a large saucepan and fry the paste, stirring constantly, until golden brown.
- Add the coriander, cumin, chilli, Garam Masala and stir-fry for 1 to 2 minutes.
- Add salt to taste.
- Then add the lamb and fry for a few minutes.
- Add the yoghurt, mix well and fry for a further minute.
- Add the double cream, mix well and fry for a further minute.
- Add the water and when it starts to boil, lower the heat.
- Cover and cook for about 40 minutes, stirring occasionally.
- Finally add the tomatoes, stir well to mix, cover again and cook for a further 25 - 30 minutes until the lamb is tender and the gravy slightly thickened.
- For garnishing, add some freshly chopped coriander

Shea's Curried Sausages

Using a Large Wok, Put Oil in Wok

Cut Sausages into Small Lengths

Brown Sausages

Remove from Wok

Cut up Onion/Carrots/Mushrooms

Fry these ingredients until the Onion is Soft

Add Maggie Curried Sausages Mix

Add 310mls Water

Add One Tin of Peeled Tomatoes

Stir in and bring to the Boil

Then add Browned Sausages in Stir

Then turn down to a Simmer and Stirring Mixture occasionally

Cook for 25 minutes

Cooking with Shea

Chicken Curry

By Charmaine Solomon

Ingredients

1.5kg chicken thigh cutlets
2 tbsp ghee or vegetable oil
¼ tsp fenugreek seeds
10 curry leaves
2 large onions, finely chopped
4-5 cloves garlic, finely chopped
2 tsp fresh ginger, finely grated
1 tsp turmeric powder
1 tsp chilli powder
1 tbsp ground coriander
½ tsp ground fennel
1 tsp cumin
2 tsp paprika
2 tsp salt
2 tbsp vinegar
2 tomatoes, peeled and chopped
6 cardamom pods, bruised
1 stick cinnamon
1 stalk lemon grass
1 pandan leaf
1 cup thick coconut milk

Preparation

Heat ghee and fry fenugreek and curry leaves until they start to brown.

Add onions, garlic and ginger and fry gently until onions are quite soft and transparent.

Add turmeric, chilli, coriander, cumin, fennel, paprika, salt and vinegar and stir well.

Add tomatoes, whole spices and lemon grass.

Add chicken and stir over medium heat until chicken is thoroughly coated with spices. Cook, covered, over low heat for 40 to 50 minutes.

Add coconut milk, taste and add more salt and a squeeze of lemon juice if desired.

Do not cover after adding coconut milk.

Serve with stringhoppers or rice and coconut sambol.

If you enjoyed this Chicken curry recipe then browse more sri lankan recipes, curry recipes, meat recipes and our most popular salt and pepper squid recipe.

Cooking with Shea

FISH RECIPES

Shea's Baked Trout

BAKED FISH IN FOIL

1 or 2 lg. sea trout, stripe bass or rainbow trout
1 each green & red pepper, chopped
1 onion, sliced
1-2 garlic cloves, sliced
Salt to taste
1/2 tsp. black pepper
1/2 tsp. white pepper
1/4 c. butter, sliced
Foil
1/4 c. water
1/2 tsp. paprika

Line a baking dish with foil; add water under foil. Wash fish. Season with black and white pepper, salt, paprika. Place fish in foil.

Top with peppers and onion. Top this with butter. Cover with foil.

Bake in a 350°F oven for about 20 to 25 minutes. Fish should be flaky with a nice soft touch.

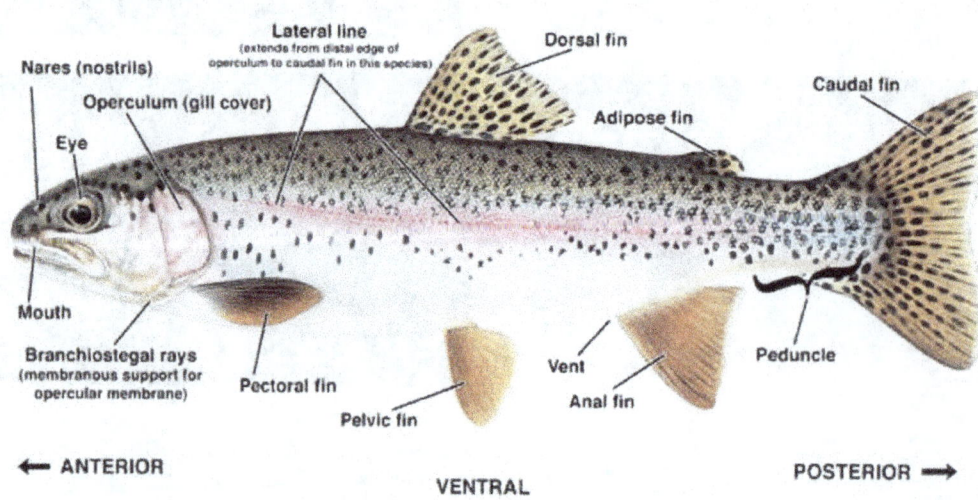

Cooking with Shea

PICKLED HERRINGS

2 X 300GRM (240) GRM PACKET – MATJES HERRING FILLETS – SLICED IN THICK STRIPS

2 x Red Onions – Finely Chopped

1 Apple Peeled and Grated

8 Black Peppercorns + 6 Cloves (Ground Mortar Pestle)

4 Bay Leaves (Take out before you serve)

2 Tbsps White Wine Vinegar

1 Cup (250ml) Yoghurt Plain-Thick

3 Tbsps Sour Cream

50ml Milk (only if required)

Pumpernickel Bread

Preparation

Sliced Herrings in non metallic bowl – add onions, apple, spices, vinegar, yoghurt, sour cream to give herrings thick coating

Gently combine and season with pepper (if required)
Serve on pumpernickel

Cooking with Shea

Ingredients (serves 4)

- 500g potatoes (such as pontiac or desiree), peeled
- 440g can red salmon
- 1 small onion, peeled, grated
- 2 celery sticks, finely chopped
- 1 tbs chopped fresh dill
- 1 tsp grated lemon rind
- 20ml (1 tbs) lemon juice
- 2 eggs, lightly beaten
- 40ml (2 tbs) milk
- 1/2 cup plain flour
- 2 cups fresh breadcrumbs
- Sunflower (or similar) oil, to fry
- Mayonnaise, to serve

Method

1. Cut the potatoes into rough chunks. Boil or steam until tender, then mash until smooth. Transfer to a large bowl to cool.
2. Drain the salmon and remove any bones. Add to the potatoes with the onion, celery, dill and lemon rind and juice. Season with salt and pepper. Mix well together, then use your hands to form into 8 patties. Refrigerate for 30 minutes.
3. Beat together the eggs and milk in a bowl. Place flour and breadcrumbs in separate bowls. Dip each patty in the flour, then in the egg mixture and lastly in the breadcrumbs. Heat the oil in a heavy-based saucepan over medium-high heat. Add patties (in batches) and fry both sides until golden brown. Serve with a dollop of mayonnaise and the cucumber salad.

JAMIE OLIVER'S FABULOUS FISH CAKES

This is one of Jamie's 'Feed Your Family for a Fiver' recipes from Sainsbury's Try Something New Today.

They were very easy to make and instead of my usual method of cooking fish cakes in butter and oil in a frying pan, these were cooked in the oven with only a drizzle of oil over them and obviously this is a much healthier option.

The basics salmon was surprisingly good, and I wouldn't hesitate to use this again in recipes requiring cooked salmon. Make sure you go over the salmon though for the odd few bones because you wouldn't want your children to have any of these in their mouths!

Nigel Slater says tinned salmon makes 'deeply flavoured fish cakes'. He has written a charming piece about fish cakes for Waitrose.

Here is Jamie's recipe:

Serves: 4

You will need: 350g basics salmon fillets, 4 baking potatoes, 1 lemon, 1 egg

1. Place the salmon fillets in a metal colander over a pan of simmering water. cover and steam for 5 minutes.

2. Peel the 4 potatoes, cut each into about 8 pieces and boil until soft. Mash and leave to cool. Remove any skin from the salmon, flake and mix with the potatoes, a lightly whisked egg, lemon zest and some salt and pepper. Roll the mixture into 8 fish cakes.

3. Drizzle olive oil on both sides of the fish cakes and cook on a baking tray in a preheated oven for 15 minutes at 200°C/Fan 180°C/Gas 6 or until crispy on the outside and heated through.

For the salad: Round lettuce, cucumber portion, 2 tomatoes, 1 red onion.

1. Quarter the heart of the lettuce and set aside.

2. Chop all the remaining washed salad ingredients, including the outer lettuce leaves.

3. Place in a salad bowl.

For the dressing: Dijon mustard, juice of the lemon, olive oil, salt and pepper.

1. Make a well in the middle of the prepared salad and squeeze in the juice of the lemon. Add a dash of olive oil, a spoonful of Dijon mustard and the salt and pepper.

2. Mix through the salad.

3. Serve the fish cakes with the salad and quartered lettuce heart.

Cooking with Shea

Crisp Honey Prawns

Lightly battered and pan-fried, these prawns are coated in a delicious sticky and sweet honey that will be popular with the whole family.

Cooking with Shea

Ingredients

SERVES 4

- 2 tsp cornflour
- 2 egg whites
- 2 tsp oyster sauce
- 3 tbsp vegetable oil
- 3 tbsp plain flour
- sea salt, to taste
- freshly ground black pepper
- 20 raw prawns, peeled and deveined, tails intact
- ½ cup honey
- ½ cup roughly chopped coriander

SERVING SUGGESTION

Serve with a simple salad of sliced vine tomatoes and red onions drizzled with a little olive oil and balsamic vinegar.

Nutritional information per serving: kilojoules 6161/calories 1467, fat 109.2g (sat fat 66.2g), carbs 86.3g

Easy Step-by-Step

1. Combine the cornflour, egg whites and oyster sauce in a bowl. Use a whisk to beat the mixture together until thickened.

2. Heat oil in a nonstick frying pan over medium heat. Put flour in a bowl and season. Dip prawns, several at a time, into the flour, shaking off any excess, then dip into batter mixture to coat. Cook in the pan for 2 minutes on each side until golden. Put cooked prawns on paper towel to absorb excess oil while preparing and cooking the remaining prawns.

3. Discard oil once all of the prawns have been cooked. Add the honey to the pan and cook over low heat for 1 minute or until runny. Add the prawns and gently toss to coat in the honey. Sprinkle over the coriander and serve immediately.

Great Ideas

If you like, you can add garlic to the dish for extra flavour. Add some crushed garlic to the batter in Step 1.

© MMVII International Masters Publishers AB. Mealtimes Made Easy. AU C600 20000/4

Cooking with Shea

Italian Food

Shea's Pizza

Pepperoni
Cherry Tomatoes
Anchovies
Onion
Olives
Bocconcini Cheese
Tomato Paste
Grated Parmesan Cheese
Pizza Base from Harris Farm

Preheat Oven 210°C fan forced
Cook for 15 to 17 mins

Shea's Lasagne

Ingredients

Lasagne Sheets

Beef Mince
Prosciutto
Bacon

Broccoli
Eggplant
Celery
Carrot
Onion
Garlic
Oregano
Parsley
Basil

Red Wine
Tomato Paste
Peeled Tomatoes

Parmesan Cheese
Mozzarella Cheese

Béchamel Sauce

Heat Oil in large pot and add Onion, Bacon, Garlic and cook until soft. Then add chopped up Eggplant, Celery, Carrot cook until soft. Add Mince cook until brown. Add Peeled Tomatoes and Broccoli and Oregano and Basil then mix in well. Add Tomato Paste stir in thoroughly. Then add Red Wine to cover ingredients. Simmer covered for 45 minutes, simmer uncovered for 15 minutes or until liquid has almost evaporated.

Place one layer of Lasagne Sheets on the bottom of dish then a layer of Lasagne Mix then Béchamel Sauce, then a layer of Lasagne sheets then a layer of Lasagne Mix then a layer of Prosciutto then Béchamel Sauce then a layer of Lasagne Sheets then a layer of Béchamel sauce and cheeses on top. Sprinkle with Parsley. Cook in a preheated oven at 180°C for 45minutes, then check. Cook for a further 15minutes if necessary.

Cooking with Shea

SHEA'S TUNA PASTA BAKE

Ingredients

250 g tomato paste

1 pkt MAGGI Bakes Tuna Pasta Bake Recipe Mix

1 can tuna in spring water, drained, 185g

3 1/2 cups water

250 g dried penne pasta

1/2 cup grated tasty cheese

Method

1. Preheat oven to 200°C/180°C. fan forced

2. Add combined tomato paste, MAGGI Bakes Tuna Pasta Bake Recipe Mix, tuna and water to pan. Bring to boil stirring.

3. Place uncooked pasta in ovenproof dish (2.5L capacity), cover with mixture stirring to combine. Bake covered for 20 minutes. Stir.

4. Sprinkle evenly with grated cheese. Bake uncovered 15 minutes or until golden brown.

5. Serve with a garden salad.

Tomato, spinach & bocconini omelette pizza

Cooking with Shea

Tomato, spinach & bocconini omelette pizza

Preparation 15 mins | Cooking 5 mins | Serves 2-4

6 free-range eggs
1 tbs water
30g baby spinach leaves, finely chopped + extra leaves to serve
olive oil cooking spray
200g tomato medley or cherry tomatoes, halved
100g bocconcini, drained and sliced

STEP 1 Preheat a grill on medium-high heat. Crack eggs into a medium bowl. Add water and whisk until foaming. Stir in spinach.

STEP 2 Spray a 23cm base non-stick ovenproof frying pan with oil to grease. Heat over medium-high heat. Add eggs and swirl to coat base of the pan. Shake the pan over heat, cooking until eggs are almost set. When almost set (but still runny on the top), scatter with tomatoes and bocconcini.

STEP 3 Place pan under the preheated grill and cook until egg is set. Turn pizza omelette onto a board. Sprinkle with extra spinach leaves and serve.

Good for you...*SPINACH*

Although the iron in spinach is not well absorbed, its high content of vitamins C, E, beta carotene (converts to vitamin A in the body), niacin (B3), folate, vitamin B6 plus its magnesium and potassium make it one of the most valuable vegetables. Spinach is rich in an antioxidant called lutein, which is important for eye health.

Cooking with Shea

LAMB RECIPES

Shea's Roast Lamb Shoulder

1.5 Kgs
3 HOUR COOKING TIME
Fan Forced Oven
1 ½ HOURS @ 160°C + 1 ½ HOURS @ 140°C

1.5 kg	Lamb Shoulder with shank intact
1 ½ tbls	Olive Oil
30g	Butter
1kg	Potatoes, sliced thinly
2	Medium Brown Onions (300g) sliced thinly
4	Drained anchovy fillets, chopped finely
2	Bulbs Garlic
2tbls	Fresh Rosemary Leaves
2cups 500ml	Water or Red Wine
	Plum Jam and Honey

1. Preheat oven to 180 °C/160 °C fan forced
2. Heat Plum Jam and Honey in small pot to just melted.
3. Pour over lamb before putting the lamb into the oven.
4. Place Lamb Shoulder into Baking Dish then sprinkle Lamb with rosemary and garlic and anchovies, add the water or red wine to baking dish. Pour Jam and Honey Mixture over Lamb. Cover dish tightly with two layers of foil.
5. **Roast 1 ½ hours at 180 °C convention/160 °C fan forced.**
6. Remove foil. **Reduce the oven temperature to 160 °C convention/140 °C fan forced; Roast further 1 ½ hours.**
7. Remove lamb, cover; **stand 10 minutes.**
8. Serve lamb with potatoes and half a bulb of garlic.

Put the vegetables on a separate tray for 1 ½ hours at 140 °C. This time includes the resting time of Lamb Shoulder.

Heat Plum Jam and Honey in small pot and pour over lamb before putting the lamb into the oven.

Cooking with Shea

SHEA'S Pot-Roasted Lamb Shanks

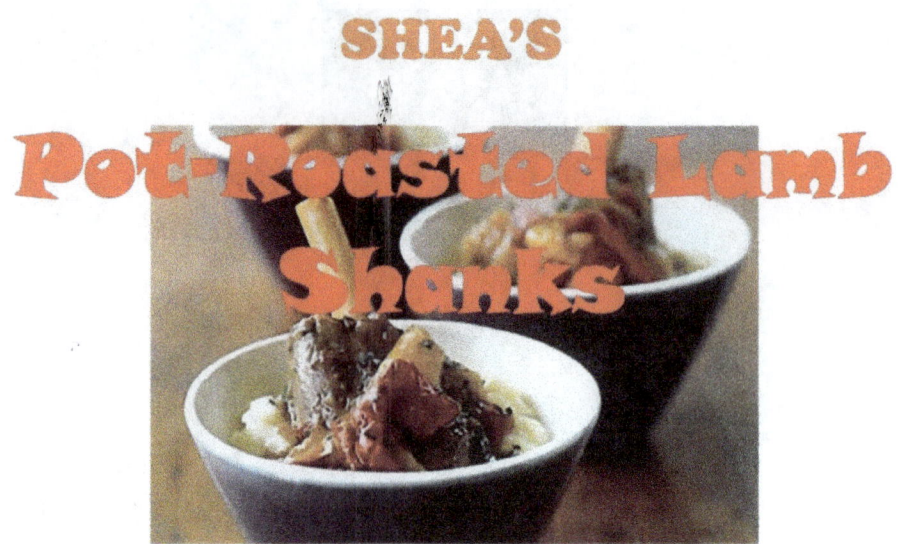

Ingredients (serves 6)

- 1 tbs olive oil
- 6 frenched lamb shanks
- 2 red onions, sliced
- 2 red capsicum, seeds removed, thickly sliced
- 2 yellow capsicum, seeds removed, thickly sliced
- 6 garlic cloves, crushed
- 300ml white wine
- 3 tbs sundried tomato pesto
- 2 cups (500ml) lamb or beef stock
- 10 vine-ripened tomatoes, quartered
- Leaves of 1 long sprig rosemary
- 2 tbs chopped flat-leaf parsley
- Creamy mashed potato, to serve

Method

1. Preheat the oven to 180°C.
2. Heat the oil in a large ovenproof casserole over high heat and brown lamb shanks in batches to seal on all sides. Remove and set aside.
3. Reduce heat to medium and add onion, capsicum and garlic to the casserole. Cook, stirring, for about 5 minutes until vegetables start to soften.
4. Add wine, pesto and stock, then return shanks to pan. Add tomato and rosemary and season with salt and pepper. Bring to the boil, cover, and roast in oven for 2 1/2 hours. Remove lid and cook for a further hour. Stir in parsley, reserving a little to garnish.
5. To serve, dollop mash into 6 deep bowls, sit a shank on top and spoon around some sauce and vegetables. Garnish with parsley.

Shea's Roast Lamb

Ingredients

1.5 kg Lamb Leg
Rosemary
Garlic
Honey
Pepper
Oil
Red Wine
Beef Stock Cube and Water

Combine Rosemary, Garlic, Pepper, Oil in a bowl.
Place Leg of Lamb into Tupperware Bowl.
Pour in Red Wine and Beef Stock over Lamb.
Rub Lamb with the ingredients mixed in a bowl.
Pour spoonfuls of Honey over Lamb.
Allow Lamb to marinade over night in the Refrigerator.

Preheat Oven to 200°c fan forced
Shake Tupperware to cover Lamb with Marinade
Place Lamb on Rack in Baking Dish
Add Water to Dish

Place Lamb into the Preheated Oven 200°c

Cooking Time for Lamb

Cook Lamb at 200°c for 48 minutes

Then reduce temperature to 180°c

Cook Lamb at 180°c for 47 minutes

Rest Lamb for 10 minutes

Cooking Time for Vegetables

Place vegetables in the Oven at 180°c and cook for 57 minutes

Gravy

**Mix 3 Heaped Desert Spoonfuls of Gravox Gravy Mix (Lamb and Rosemary) in pot with Boiling Water.
Heat on Stove Hotplate stirring constantly until bubbling hot.**

Shea's Roast Lamb

2.7 kilos Lamb Leg

160°C Fan Forced

Cook for

2 hours 45 minutes

Vegetables

Place vegetables in the oven
For the last
1 hour of cooking

Cooking with Shea

Shea's Braised Lamb Shoulder Chops
Cooked in a 6.3litre Dutch Oven

Use your favourite dry red wine to flavour these comforting lamb shoulder chops. The chops are browned then braised in red wine along with a complementary combination of onions, rosemary, and garlic. The long, slow, oven braising ensures tender, melt-in-your-mouth lamb chops.

Ingredients

3 tablespoons olive oil (divided)

- 2 medium onions (halved, sliced to 1/4-inch thickness)
- 4 to 6 lamb shoulder chops
- 4 cloves garlic (minced)
- 1 cup dry red wine (such as a Cabernet or Pinot)
- 3 tablespoons Dijon mustard or Wholegrain Mustard (good-quality,
- or similar gourmet mustard)
- 1 teaspoon salt
- 1/2 teaspoon freshly ground black pepper
- 1 tablespoon fresh rosemary (chopped) or more rosemary if you deserve (whole).
-
- **Steps to Cook It**

1. Heat the oven to **300F. or 149C fan forced oven.**
2. Put 2 tablespoons of olive oil and the sliced onions in a heavy 6.3 litre Baccarat Dutch Oven or stew pot over medium heat.
3. Cook the onions, stirring frequently, until lightly browned. Remove to a plate.
4. Add the remaining olive oil and the chops—in batches, if necessary —and cook, turning until nicely browned on both sides, about 3 to 4 minutes on each side.
5. Add the garlic and cook for 1 more minute.
6. Add the onions back to the pot with the lamb and garlic.
7. In a bowl or 2-cup measuring cup, combine the dry red wine with the mustard, salt, pepper, and rosemary. Blend well with spoon or whisk.
8. Pour over the lamb mixture.
9. If the pot isn't oven-safe, move everything to a large baking pan or casserole. Cover the pot or pan tightly with a lid or foil.
10. Braise in the convention or fan-forced oven for 2 hours and check for tenderness or 3 hours if preferred or until the lamb chops are very tender.
11. Serve the lamb chops with the cooking juices, mashed potatoes, and cabbage, or another side vegetable, along with warm biscuits or a hearty bread.

SHEA'S
Plum and Rosemary Lamb Shanks

Ingredients (serves 4)

- 2 tablespoons plain flour
- 8 small French-trimmed lamb shanks
- (see note)
- 1 ½ tablespoons olive oil
- 1 brown onion, halved, thinly sliced
- ¼ cup fresh rosemary leaves
- 1 tablespoon fresh thyme leaves
- 1 cup red wine
- 1 ½ cups chicken stock
- 2 tablespoons Worcestershire sauce
- 1 cup plum jam
- mashed potato and steamed green beans, to serve

Method

1. Preheat oven to 200°C/180°C fan-forced. Place flour and shanks in a bowl. Toss to coat. Heat 2 tablespoons oil in a large, heavy-based, flameproof casserole dish over high heat. Cook shanks, turning, in batches, for 4 to 5 minutes or until browned. Transfer to a plate.
2. Reduce heat to medium-high. Heat remaining oil in casserole. Add onion, rosemary and thyme. Cook for 3 to 4 minutes or until onion is tender. Add wine. Simmer for 1 minute. Stir in stock, sauce and jam. Season with pepper. Add shanks. Bring to the boil. Cover dish. Transfer to oven.
3. Bake for 1 hour. Remove lid and baste shanks. Bake, uncovered, for 30 to 40 minutes or until meat is tender and falling from the bone. Serve with mash and beans.

BRAISED LAMB SHANKS

INGREDIENTS

750g Greek natural yoghurt
4 lamb shanks, trimmed
Salt & freshly ground black pepper
Olive oil
¼ cup white wine
1 1/2 cups chicken stock
2 French shallots, peeled, thinly sliced
2 whole garlic cloves
6 sprigs thyme
1 lemon, rind peeled into strips, halved
5 beads mastic
2 tbs honey
Extra virgin olive oil
Young sprigs flat leaf parsley, to serve

Serves 4

1. Spoon the yoghurt into a fine meshed sieve and place over a bowl. Cover and refrigerate overnight to allow excess liquid to drain from the yoghurt.

2. Preheat oven 165 degrees celsius conventional/140 degress celsius fan forced. Heat a large deep ovenproof frying pan over high heat until hot. Season shanks well with salt and pepper. Cover the base of the pan with oil and cook shanks, in two batches, for 5 minutes, turning until golden all over. Return all shanks to pan and deglaze the pan with the wine. Pour in the chicken stock. Remove pan from the heat.

3. Spoon the yoghurt over the lamb to cover. Scatter over the shallots, garlic, thyme, lemon rind, mastic and drizzle with honey. Place a cartouche (round of baking paper) onto the surface of the lamb and cover with a light fitting lid. Transfer to the oven and cook for 4 hours.

4. Remove the lid, cartouche and sprigs of thyme. Carefully transfer the lamb to a warm serving platter and spoon over some of the thick yoghurt top. Strain the juices into a saucepan and bring to simmer over medium heat. Squeeze in the juice from half lemon. Remove from heat, insert a stick blender into the sauce and while blending add 2-3 tbs extra virgin olive oil. Taste and season with salt and pepper. Pour the sauce over the lamb, scatter with parsley and serve.

BAKED LAMB CHOPS "ITALIAN"

Italian Grandmother's are great. I happen to have one, and they seem to have a long running tradition of being pretty handy in the kitchen. That, and making sure you eat, because to them, *everyone* looks like they are starving.

I don't have too many memories of cooking with my grandmother, since we lived about 2,000 miles away most of my childhood. But I do know she made a killer homemade gnocchi. And in return, I subjected her to my version of peach pie when I was 12 years old- A can of peaches, the juice cooked & thickened with corn starch, dumped into a store-bought crust, and baked. But she was very supportive of my endeavors.

Another great thing about Italian Grandmothers, they don't pay too much attention to pesky things like whether you are related to them or not. So while I did not get too much time in the kitchen with my own grandmother, I knew a few through various family friends and church events.

At one such church event, I met a little Italian grandmother that made this heavenly dish of baked lamb chops. Delicate, juicy, and layered with more onions, tomatoes, and garlic than you can shake a fist at. And she was nice enough to take pity on my 14 year old culinary self, and wrote down the recipe for me.

Cooking with Shea

15 years later, I have this recipe committed to memory, and it is my 'go to' recipe anytime I want to wow someone. Or if I want to spoil my dad when he's out to visit. Or pretty much any time I feel like I need a little grandmotherly love.

Cast of Characters:
This is pretty straightforward in the ingredient department. Other than the chops, everything else can be found in most any kitchen - sliced onion, chopped garlic, sliced tomatoes, grated Romano (or parmigiana, both work well) cheese, olive oil, salt (table works as well as sea), pepper, and Italian seasoning (or your own mix of dried basil/oregano/etc).

For the chops themselves, I've learned to try not to be too picky. Most grocery stores carry lamb chops in a limited selection, and I'll grab whatever looks good. These petite loin chops would be my first choice since they are lower in fat and gristle, and the thickness lends a nice juiciness to the dish. If loin chops aren't available, I'd recommend some shoulder round chops or rib chops. I wouldn't recommend the shoulder chops because they are pretty riddled in bone and gristle, and pretty hard to cut up and eat when layered under all the tomato-ey goodness.

Assembly:
So... to assemble this, we do it in three repetitive layers, plus a layer of chops. Depending on the size of your chop, I usually allot for 2-3 per person. So we want to pick a baking dish large enough to fit them all. Snug fitting is fine, they will shrink a bit as they bake. First we start by drizzling the pan with about 1/4 cup of olive oil. Lamb can be a fatty meat, so less is more with the oil. I usually use my pampered chef pump spritzer for this.

Cooking with Shea

Next, layer in 1/3 of the tomatoes. A nice even layer, allotting for at least one slice under each chop, or just evenly spread about.

Next, we add 1/3 of the sliced onions, and 1/3 the chopped garlic. The more the better as they definitely add a punch of flavor to the dish.

Finally, we add a liberal dash of the Romano cheese, salt, pepper and Italian seasoning.

On top of this, lay the chops.

Repeat the oil - through - seasoning layers.

Repeat them one last time. The more the better here, the less you can see of the chop, the better.

Now, take this multi layer wonder and put it in the oven at 350 deg f for 40 minutes. Set about making some risotto, and try not to gain 20 lbs simply smelling the chops as they meld with all the flavor.

After 40 minutes, we're not quite done. Take out the chops, and turn the oven up to 375 deg f. Now we want to drizzle the chops with some white wine. The Nice Italian grandmother wrote 1/4 a cup, but honestly, I just drizzle straight out of the bottle, whatever you have in the house. This week I happen to have cooking wine. We're more of a red wine drinking household, so I usually keep white cooking wine on hand. But whatever white you have on hand is fine. Heck, I've used Saki in a pinch, and it still tasted great.

Cooking with Shea

After a healthy drizzle pop the chops back in the oven for 15 minutes.

NOW they are ready.
Serve with a spatula to get up as many of the 'extras' with each chop. The baking has made them all meld into a melt in your mouth nirvana of flavor.

Enjoy. And try not to eat the whole pan on your own. Maybe invite your own italian grandmother over, and make her proud.

Italian Baked Lamb Chops

Ingredients
4 Lamb Chops
3 Tbs Olive Oil
3-4 Cloves Garlic, Chopped
1 md Onion, sliced
2 Tomatoes, sliced
3 Tsp Italian Seasoning Blend
3 Tsp Salt
3 Tsp fresh Ground Pepper
1/2 c Grated Romano Cheese
1/4 c White Wine

Cooking with Shea

Directions

1. Preheat Oven to 350 deg F
2. This recipe is done in three layers of ingredients, construct in the following order: Drizzle a glass baking dish with 1 Tbs Olive Oil, 1/3 of the Chopped Garlic, 1/3 of the Sliced Onion, 1/3 of the Sliced Tomatoes, 1/3 of the Italian Seasoning, Salt, Pepper, and Romano Cheese.
3. Lay the chops flat on this first layer of ingredients, then repeat the Oil, Garlic, Onion, Tomatoes, Seasonings and Cheese twice for a total of three layers altogether.
4. Bake at 350 deg for 40 minutes, then drizzle with 1/4 cup White Wine. Increase heat to 375 deg, and cook an additional 15 minutes.
5. Serve with a spatula to get as many of the extra ingredients with the chop as possible, and enjoy.

Cooking with Shea

(1kg) (8) Lean Lamb Chops or Cutlets

1 Onion sliced

2 Carrots sliced

½ cup Peas

Maggi Lamb Ragout packet mix

Stove Top

Heat 1tbsp oil in pan, brown lamb, add onion and carrots, cook 2 minutes.

Add combined 1 ¼ cups (310ml) water, and Maggi Recipe Base, bring to boil, stirring.

Cover and simmer 30 minutes or until lamb is tender, stir occasionally, add peas, simmer 2 minutes.

Serve with potato and steamed vegetables.

Oven

Preheat oven to 180°c/160°c fan forced.

Place lamb, onion and carrots in ovenproof dish.

\Stir in combined 1 cup (250ml) water and Maggi Recipe Base, cover.

Bake 1 ½ hours or until lamb is tender, stir twice during cooking. Stir in peas during second stirring.

Serve with potato and steamed vegetables.

Cooking with Shea

roast leg of lamb with gravy

PREPARATION TIME 10 MINUTES • COOKING TIME 2 HOURS

When you prepare this recipe, you'll understand why some people would give up a date with Tom Cruise rather than miss out on a home-cooked roast. Making a scrumptious roast is just a matter of following a few tried and tested rules and not trying to improve on perfect.

1 bunch fresh rosemary
2kg leg of lamb
2 cloves garlic, each cut into 8 slices
1/4 cup olive oil (60ml)
40g butter
1 small brown onion (80g), chopped finely
2 tablespoons plain flour
1/2 cup dry red wine (125ml)
1 1/2 cups lamb or beef stock (375ml)

1 Preheat oven to hot.

2 Cut 16 similar-size rosemary sprigs from bunch; place remainder of bunch in large flameproof baking dish.

3 Remove and discard as much excess fat from lamb as possible. Pierce surface of lamb all over, making 16 small cuts with a sharp knife; press garlic slices and rosemary sprigs into cuts.

4 Place lamb on top of rosemary in baking dish. Pour oil over the lamb; roast, uncovered, in hot oven 20 minutes. Reduce temperature to moderate; roast lamb, occasionally spooning pan juices over, another 1 1/2 hours. Remove lamb from pan; stand 5 minutes before slicing.

5 Drain juices from pan, melt butter in pan over low heat; cook onion, stirring, until soft. Stir in flour; cook, stirring, about 5 minutes or until browned. Pour in wine and stock; cook over high heat, stirring, until gravy boils and thickens. Strain gravy; serve with lamb.

SERVES 6

per serve 26.3g fat; 2038kJ

Studding lamb with garlic and rosemary

Spooning pan juices over lamb

Browning flour for gravy

tips

- Try substituting fresh lemon thyme, mint or flat-leaf parsley for the rosemary.
- Rest the roast, covered in foil, 10 to 15 minutes before carving so that the juices "settle". When carving the roast, slice across the grain – the meat is more tender this way.
- For the stock, make your own (substituting lamb bones for beef in our beef stock recipe on page 116), use a commercially prepared version or combine 1 cup of boiling water with 1 crumbled stock cube or 1 teaspoon stock powder.
- We used red shiraz in this recipe but any dry red wine can be used.
- The gravy recipe can easily be adapted into either a peppercorn or mushroom gravy. Return strained gravy to a clean saucepan then add either 1 tablespoon of drained, rinsed, canned green peppercorns or 100g finely sliced cooked button mushrooms to gravy. Cook, stirring, 2 minutes; serve.

PORK RECIPES

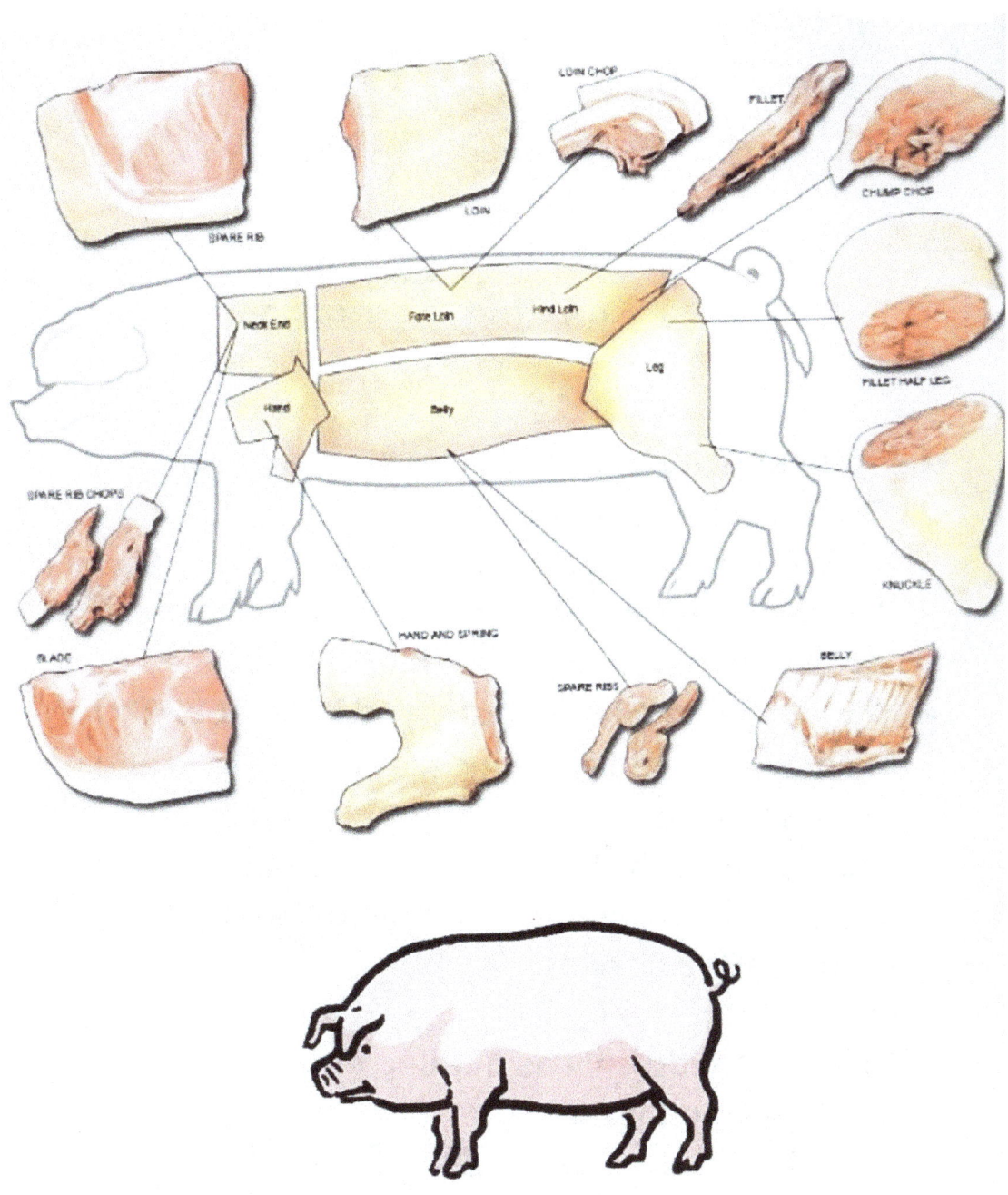

Australian Pork Roast Leg

Boneless Pork Leg Roast

Easy Roasting Instructions

1. Preheat oven to 220°c.
2. Remove plastic bag and soaker pad.
3. For perfect crackling wipe rind with paper towel to dry, then rub two tablespoons of salt and two tablespoons of oil into the rind.
4. Place roast in a baking tray and bake at 220°c for 20 minutes then reduce temperature to 180°c and bake for 40 minutes per kilogram.
5. Once cooked thoroughly or as desired, remove from oven and allow the rest for 10 minutes and remove string before carving.

Use as a guide only as heating efficiencies of appliances may vary.

SHEA'S ROAST PORK

2 KILOGRAMS or 4.5 LBS

30 MINUTES PER POUND

500 (F) or 260 © for 30 or 45 minutes
350 (F) or 180 © for the rest of the cooking time

POTATOES

2 HOURS 6 MINUTES at 350 (F)

VEGETABLES

1 HOUR AT 350 (F)

Rosemary Roasted Pork

INGREDIENTS

1.8 kg Rolled Pork Loin
¼ Cup Rosemary Leaves
2 tbls Sea Salt Flakes
Olive Oil for drizzling

Preheat oven to 220°c. Using a sharp knife, score the pork skin. Secure the loin with kitchen string and place in a baking dish lined with non-stick baking paper. Place the rosemary and salt in a small frying pan over high heat and cook for 1-2 minutes or until fragrant. Process the mixture in a small food processor until well combined and rub onto the pork skin. Drizzle over the oil. Roast the pork for 30 minutes then reduce the heat to 180°c and roast for a further hour. Slice and serve with the thyme-roasted vegetables and maple apple sauce.

THYME-ROASTED VEGETABLES

650G Sweet Potato, quartered
2 Red Onions, quartered
2 Parsnips, peeled and halved
1 head garlic, cloves separated
6 Sprigs of Thyme
¼ Cup Olive Oil
Sea Salt Flakes

Preheat oven to 180°c. Place the sweet potato, onion, parship, garlic, thyme, oil and salt in a baking dish lined with non-stick baking paper and toss to combine. Roast the vegetables for 1 hour or until cooked and golden.
Tip: Place the vegetables in the oven during the pork's last hour of cooking.

Cooking with Shea

Shea's Pork Hocks

Ingredients

1 kg Pork Hocks (2 portions)
2 tbsp Salt
Garlic
Oil

Brandy

Red Wine

Oranges peeled and sliced

Woolworths Black Stoneless Cherries

Marjoram / Oil / Lemon Juice

Orange Marmalade

Honey

Butter

Thyme

Caraway Seeds

Pepper

Place Pork Hocks in Tupperware Container.

Pour into bottom of Tupperware Container a tin of Stoneless Black Cherries and Red Wine.

Rub Pork Hocks with crushed garlic, salt, oil.

Mix Marjoram/Oil/Lemon Juice together then pour over Pork Hocks.

Sprinkle Thyme, Carraway Seeds, Pepper over Hocks.

Then put into Refrigerator to Marinade over night.

Place a thick layer of Orange Slices in the bottom of an oven proof pyrex dish.

Place Pork Hocks on the top of the Orange Slice layer.

Pour into the bottom of dish remaining Marinade from Tupperware Container.

Pour brandy gently over Hocks

Heat in a small pot Orange Marmalade, Honey, Butter then pour over Hocks.

Cover the whole dish with Alfoil.

Oven Temperature (150 c) Fan Forced

Place in the middle shelf of oven and cook for 2½ hours covered with alfoil. Then remove alfoil and cook for a further 1½ hours.

Cooking with Shea

Glazed Ham

Camps Maple Syrup

Mango Nectar

Breakfast Marmalade

Honey

Cooking with Shea

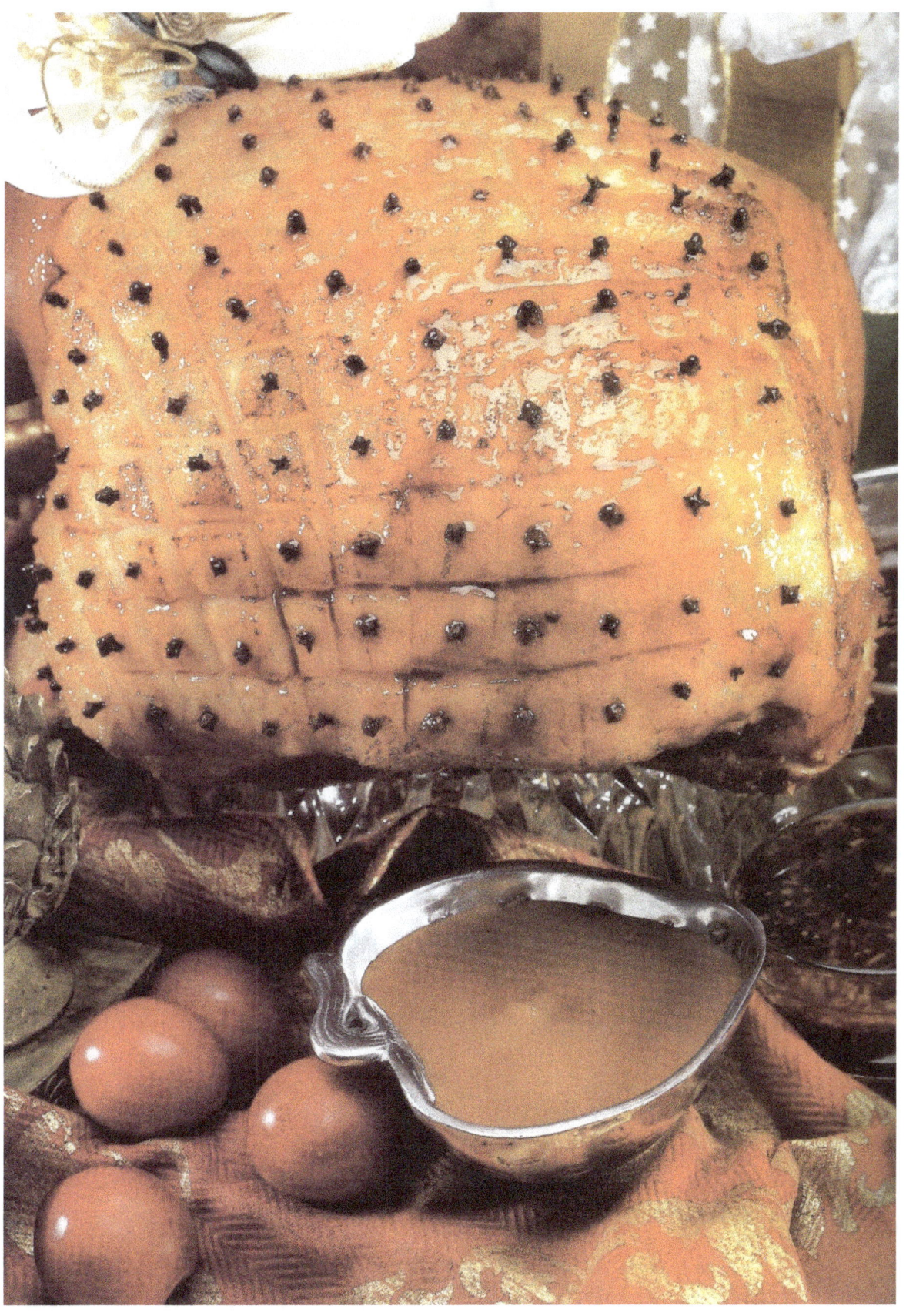

Cooking with Shea

CELEBRATION

GLAZED HAM

Most people prefer buying a cooked leg of ham and glazing it themselves about an hour before serving time. All of the following glazes can be made up to a week before using and stored, covered, in the refrigerator; none is suitable to freeze. Ham itself can be frozen for up to 8 weeks but should be glazed just before baking.

**8kg cooked leg of ham
whole cloves**

Make a decorative cut through ham rind about 10cm from shank end of leg; run thumb under edge of rind at other end of leg then, using fingers to loosen it, pull rind away from the fat. Continue to carefully pull rind away from fat until you reach decorative cut at shank end; discard rind.

Make shallow cuts in one direction diagonally across fat at 2cm intervals then shallow cut diagonally in opposite direction, forming diamonds. Do not cut through surface of top fat or fat will spread, losing pattern, during cooking. Place 1 clove in centre of each diamond then position ham on wire rack in large baking dish. Wrap shank with foil; brush ham with glaze.

Bake, uncovered, in moderate oven about 50 minutes or until browned all over, brushing frequently with glaze during cooking.

MAPLE SYRUP GLAZE

1 tablespoon mustard powder
1½ cups (375ml) maple-
   flavoured syrup
⅓ cup (80ml) cider vinegar

Mix all ingredients in small bowl until powder dissolves.

REDCURRANT JELLY AND ORANGE GLAZE

½ cup (125ml) redcurrant jelly
¼ cup (60ml) port
½ cup (125ml) orange juice
½ cup (125ml) marmalade

Mix all ingredients in small pan; stir over low heat until jelly and marmalade melt. Simmer 5 minutes or until mixture thickens slightly.

MANGO GLAZE

⅔ cup (160ml) mango nectar
⅓ cup (80ml) mango chutney
¼ cup (50g) firmly packed
   brown sugar
1 tablespoon Dijon mustard

Mix all ingredients in small pan; stir over low heat until chutney melts.

APRICOT GLAZE

⅔ cup (160ml) apricot nectar
⅓ cup (80ml) apricot jam
¼ cup (50g) firmly packed
   brown sugar
1 tablespoon Dijon mustard

Mix all ingredients in small pan; stir over low heat until jam melts.

SWEET CHILLI GLAZE

⅓ cup (80ml) mild sweet chilli sauce
¼ cup (60ml) lime juice
2 teaspoons finely grated
   fresh ginger
2 tablespoons teriyaki sauce

Mix all ingredients in small bowl.

BARBECUE HONEY GLAZE

¼ cup (60ml) barbecue sauce
¼ cup (60ml) Worcestershire sauce
¼ cup (60ml) tomato sauce
¼ cup (60ml) honey

Mix all ingredients in small pan; stir over low heat until honey melts.

*CLOCKWISE FROM TOP: Redcurrant Jelly and Orange Glaze; Apricot Glaze; Barbecue Honey Glaze; Mango Glaze.
CENTRE: Sweet Chilli Glaze.*

Pebble Creek - Pork Leg Roast ALDI

(2 kg)

Pre-heat the oven to 220°c. Wipe the rind of any moisture with a paper towel.

Rub the pork rind with oil then rub salt generously in the scores and into the rind.

Raising the roast allows the heat to circulate, browning it evenly.

Roast the pork in the oven for 30 minutes or until the rind begins to crackle

Reduce the oven heat to 180°c and cook a further 40 minutes per kilogram of pork or until internal temperature reaches 70-75°c.

Transfer to a plate, cover loosely with foil and rest for 10-20 minutes before carving.

Cooking with Shea

Puff Pastry Parcels

Pulled Pork

Chinese Choy Sum

Tomato Sliced

Shredded Carrot

Parsley

Pepper

Arrange ingredients together fold Puff Pastry then fork ends
Rub Extra Virgin Olive Oil over Parcel then spray with Parsley Flakes
Put into a pre heated oven 180°degrees
Cook for 30 Minutes

Cooking with Shea

Soups

SHEA'S HAM AND BEEF BONES SOUP

INGREDIENTS

Ham Bones
Beef Bones
Onions
Garlic Cloves
Galangal
Parsley
Oregano
Thyme
Vegetables

Put all the ingredients into a large boiling pot. Bring to the boil then lower heat to simmer for 2 ½ hours then put in chopped vegetables and cook until the vegetables are soft enough for you.

SHEA'S
PORK SOUP WITH CHINESE YAM

Light and sweet.
Chinese yam is sold in 2 forms: dried and fresh.

Dried chinese yam is known as huai shan while the fresh version is known as shan yao.
The dried form comes in long whitish strips and is more common in Singapore.
They are also better for simmering soups. An excellent source of carbohydrates.

Equipment
1 small clay or ceramic soup pot or double boiler
1 large pot for steaming or slow cooker

Ingredients
50g huai shan
10 chinese wolfberries
220g prime ribs
3 slices ginger
1000ml soup stock
salt & pepper

Directions
1. Wash the chinese yam and rinse the goji berries.
2. Parboil the prime ribs for 3 minutes. Drain and trim off excess fats.
3. Place the huai shan, chinese wolfberries, ginger, prime pork ribs and the soup stock into the clay pot or double boiler
4. Bring water to boil in the large pot or wok or pour boiling water in the slow cooker and place the soup pot or double-boiler half-submerged in the water
5. Steam the soup for 2 hours
6. Add the salt and pepper before serving

SHEA'S
PORK SOUP WITH 4 CHINESE HERBS

The 4 chinese herbs are lotus seeds, chinese yam, coix seeds and chinese angelica root and is known in chinese medicine as the 4 officials.

These 4 herbs are good for the stomach, it can strengthen the spleen. If you suffer from indigestion and diarrhoea, this soup should be great for you. If you have constipation, you should avoid this.

Ingredients
2.5g lotus seeds
2.5g euryale seeds
2.5g coix seeds
2.5g poria
2.5g danggui
100g fresh chinese yam
300g pork ribs
4 cups water
1 tbsp Salt
1 tbsp cooking wine

Directions
1. Wash and soak the lotus seeds, euryale seeds, coix seeds in warm water
2. Peel the chinese yam and slice thinly
3. Wash the pork ribs and parboil
4. Place the chinese yam, lotus seeds, euryale seeds, coix seeds, poria, and pork ribs into a ceramic bowl
5. Add the water until it covers the ingredients
6. Place the bowl in a steamer or big wok and steam for 20 to 30 minutes
7. Add the salt and wine before serving

Cooking with Shea

SHEA'S PORK SOUP WITH LOTUS SEEDS

It will be refreshing for summer.

Lotus seeds are usually sold in dried form. Before use, soak for about 30 minutes. Remove the brownish skins by rubbing. They usually come with the bitter pits removed. But if you are using fresh ones, remember to remove the pits.

Lotus seeds that are already skinned and pitted should also be available. It would save you a lot of preparation work.

If you prefer the pork ribs to be more tender, increase the cooking time. Do not turn up the heat.

Ingredients

300g prime pork ribs
80g lotus seeds
80g carrots
2 slices of ginger
1500 ml water

Seasonings

½ tbsp salt
1 tbsp cooking wine

Directions

1. Cut ribs into pieces. Parboil in water for about three minutes. Drain and trim away any fat or dirt.
2. Soak the lotus seeds with cold water until soft. You can cut the lotus seeds in half if desired.
3. Wash, peel and cut the carrots into small chunks slightly smaller than the pork ribs.
4. Bring the water to the boil in a large soup pot, add the pork ribs, lotus seeds, carrots and ginger.
5. Bring the Chinese pork soup to the boil again and lower the heat to a simmer.
6. Simmer for one hour.
7. Add salt and cooking wine before serving.

Directions (slow cooker version)

1. Prepare the ingredients as per steps 1 to 3 above
2. In the slow cooker, place the pork ribs, lotus seeds, carrots and ginger and add hot water.
3. Use high heat to bring the soup to the boil and then lower the heat to a simmer.
4. Add the cooking wine.
5. Simmer for 1.5 to 2 hours
6. Add salt before serving

SHEA'S CHICKEN AND CREAMED CORN SOUP

1kg (2lb)	Chicken or Chicken Pieces
2 litres (8cups)	Water
2.5cm (1in)	Piece of Green Ginger
1	Onion
4	Peppercorns
3	Sprigs of Parsley
1 tspn	Salt/Pepper
470g	Can of Creamed Corn
4 tbspns	Corn flour
4 tbspns	Water
2	Eggs
2 tbspns	Extra Water
2	Slices of Ham
5	Shallots
½ tspn	Grated Green Ginger Extra
4	Shallots
2	Rashers of Bacon
1 pkt	Maggi Chicken Noodles

The base of most Chinese Soups is a good chicken stock. A whole chicken can be used. Some of the meat, when cooked can be shredded and added to the soup, the remainder used for another meal. However, chicken pieces will serve that same purpose. You will need about 1 kg (2 lb) of chicken pieces. Economical chicken backs give good stock. Put chicken or chicken pieces into saucepan, add water, peppercorns, peeled and sliced ginger, peeled and quartered onion, parsley and salt and bacon and creamed corn and parsley. Bring to boil over medium heat, skim well to remove any scum; reduce heat and simmer gently, covered for one and a half hours. Remove any scum from top of stock, strain, reserve six cups of the stock.

Combine in large saucepan the reserved chicken stock, creamed corn, crumbled stock cubes, extra ginger, chopped shallots, salt, pepper, and sesame oil, and chicken noodles and bring to boil. Remove meat from chicken or chicken pieces, shread finely (you will need about one cup shredded chicken). Then add the chicken to the soup.

Mix corn flour to smooth paste with the four tablespoons of water, add to soup, stir until soup boils and thickens, reduce heat, simmer one minute.

Beat eggs and extra water lightly, add to soup in a thin stream, stirring well.

Add thinly sliced ham and chicken meat to soup, heat gently. Top with extra chopped shallots.

Hearty Chicken and Vegetable Soup

Ingredients (serves 6)

- 2 tablespoons olive oil
- 1 leek, halved, washed, thinly sliced
- 2 garlic cloves, crushed
- 1 large carrot, peeled, diced
- 2 sticks celery, diced
- 2 small zucchini, diced
- 1 swede or turnip, peeled, diced
- 1 1/4 cups dry soup mix, rinsed (see note)
- 8 cups chicken stock
- 1kg skinless chicken lovely legs

Method

1. Heat oil in a large saucepan over medium heat. Add leek and garlic. Cook, stirring, for 2 minutes or until soft but not coloured. Add carrot, celery, zucchini and swede. Cook for 2 minutes. Stir in soup mix, stock, chicken and 1 cup cold water. Increase heat to high. Bring to the boil.
2. Reduce heat to low. Simmer, partially covered, stirring occasionally, for 1 hour or until soup mix and vegetables are tender.
3. Remove chicken legs from soup. Allow to cool slightly. Remove meat from bones. Roughly chop chicken meat and add to soup. Season with salt and pepper. Ladle soup into warmed bowls. Serve.

Stocks

These recipes can be made up to four days ahead and kept, covered, in the refrigerator. They can also be frozen for up to three months.

beef

2kg meaty beef bones
2 medium brown onions (300g), chopped coarsely
5.5 litres water (22 cups)
2 trimmed celery stalks (200g), chopped coarsely
2 medium carrots (240g), chopped coarsely
3 bay leaves
2 teaspoons black peppercorns
3 litres water (12 cups), extra

1 Preheat oven to 200°C/180°C fan-forced.
2 Roast bones on an oven tray, uncovered, about 1 hour or until browned.
3 Combine bones and onion with the water, celery, carrot, bay leaves and peppercorns in large saucepan or boiler; bring to a boil. Reduce heat; simmer, uncovered, 3 hours, skimming surface occasionally. Add extra water; simmer, uncovered, 1 hour. Strain stock through muslin-lined sieve or colander into large heatproof bowl; discard solids. Allow stock to cool, cover; refrigerate until cold. Skim and discard surface fat before using.

- **preparation time** 10 minutes (plus cooling and refrigeration time) **cooking time** 5 hours **makes** 3.5 litres
per 1 cup (250ml) 2g total fat (0.9g saturated fat); 259kJ (62 cal); 2.3g carbohydrate; 8g protein; 1.1g fibre

chicken

2kg chicken bones
2 medium onions (300g), chopped coarsely
2 trimmed celery stalks (200g), chopped coarsely
2 medium carrots (240g), chopped coarsely
3 bay leaves
2 teaspoons black peppercorns
5 litres (20 cups) water

1 Combine ingredients in large saucepan or boiler; simmer, uncovered, 2 hours, skimming surface occasionally. Strain stock through muslin-lined sieve or colander into large heatproof bowl; discard solids. Allow stock to cool, cover; refrigerate until cold. Skim and discard surface fat before using.

- **preparation time** 10 minutes (plus cooling and refrigeration time) **cooking time** 2 hours **makes** 3.5 litres
per 1 cup (250ml) 0.6g total fat (0.2g saturated fat); 105kJ (25 cal); 2.3g carbohydrate; 1.9g protein; 1.1g fibre

fish

1.5kg fish bones
3 litres (12 cups) water
1 medium onion (150g), chopped coarsely
2 trimmed celery stalks (200g), chopped coarsely
2 bay leaves
1 teaspoon black peppercorns

1. Combine ingredients in large saucepan; simmer, uncovered, 20 minutes. Strain stock through muslin-lined sieve or colander into large heatproof bowl; discard solids. Allow stock to cool, cover; refrigerate until cold. Skim and discard surface fat before using.

- **preparation time** 5 minutes (plus cooling and refrigeration time) **cooking time** 20 minutes **makes** 2.5 litres **per 1 cup (250ml)** 0.2g total fat (0.1g saturated fat); 63kJ (15 cal); 1.1g carbohydrate; 1.9g protein; 0.6g fibre

vegetable

2 large carrots (360g), chopped coarsely
2 large parsnips (700g), chopped coarsely
4 medium onions (600g), chopped coarsely
10 trimmed celery stalks (1kg), chopped coarsely
4 bay leaves
2 teaspoons black peppercorns
6 litres (24 cups) water

1. Combine ingredients in large saucepan; simmer, uncovered, 1½ hours. Strain stock through muslin-lined sieve or colander into large heatproof bowl; discard solids. Allow stock to cool, cover; refrigerate until cold. Skim and discard surface fat before using.

- **preparation time** 10 minutes (plus cooling and refrigeration time) **cooking time** 1 hour 30 minutes **makes** 3.5 litres **per 1 cup (250ml)** 0.2g total fat (0g saturated fat); 151kJ (36 cal); 5.7g carbohydrate; 1.4g protein; 2.9g fibre

Cooking with Shea

Pumpkin soup

0:10 To Prep
0:40 To Cook
6 SERVINGS

Find out why Taste.com.au members are raving about this version of an Australian classic.

Nutrition

Energy 985kJ	Fat saturated 6.00g
Fat Total 15.00g	Carbohydrate sugars 12.00g
Carbohydrate Total 18.00g	Dietary Fibre 6.00g
Protein 5.00g	Cholesterol 21.00mg
Sodium 694.89mg	

All nutrition values are per serve.

Ingredients

- 2 tablespoons olive oil
- 1 onion, finely chopped
- 1 leek, white part only, finely sliced
- 1 garlic clove, crushed
- 1/2 teaspoon ground coriander
- 1 teaspoon ground cumin
- 1/2 teaspoon freshly grated nutmeg
- 1kg peeled pumpkin, diced
- 1 large potato, peeled, diced
- 1L Campbell's Real Stock Chicken or Vegetable
- 1/2 cup (125ml) thin cream

Method

Related Recipes

1. Heat oil in a large saucepan over low heat, add onion and leek and cook for 2-3 minutes, until softened but not coloured. Add garlic and spices and cook, stirring, for 30 seconds. Add pumpkin, potato and stock and bring to the boil. Turn heat to low, cover and simmer for 30 minutes. Allow to cool slightly, then blend in batches.
2. Return soup to pan, stir through cream and reheat gently. Season and add a little more nutmeg if desired.

Ratings & Comments

4   Julesmorgan rated this recipe at 04:19pm Sat 20th June, 2015

4.5   alexrad added this comment at 09:42pm Sat 9th May, 2015

YUMMO! This soup literally reminded me why I love pumpkin soup (haven't made it in a while!). I was like a kid with

Cooking with Shea

cake batter, having spoons of soup from the pot after I'd had my bowl and was packing it away! I think only thing I changed was I added a bit of chili powder and probably less cream (I doubled recipe but put in 3 tablespoons of thick cream)! Definitely making this again! :)

4 cooktocook added this comment at 03:21pm Fri 1st May, 2015

I would like a bit more flavour so next time I'll add more pumpkin and two cloves of garlic. I strained and put the liquid aside blended this twice so very smooth then put pumpkin and liquid back together. Wit a bit leftover I've put in the freezer.

4 soph91 added this comment at 03:33pm Wed 22nd April, 2015

Delicious soup! Loved it. So easy and great to make in bulk for the weeks lunches! Definitely making again :)

4.5 joharnett added this comment at 10:34pm Tue 21st April, 2015

Terrific recipe. Works really well with just over half the amount of nutmeg, cumin and coriander, too - adds interest and depth to the soup without tasting too recognisably 'spiced'.

Cooking with Shea

Shea's PEA + HAM SOUP

Serves 6-8
Preparation time: 15 mins
Cooking Time 2 ½ hours

INGREDIENTS:

500g McKenzie's Green Split Peas **or 250grams**
1 Large Onion, finely diced
1 clove of garlic, finely sliced **or 3 Garlic Cloves**
1 tbsp Olive Oil
3 medium Carrots, grated
3 large Celery Sticks, grated
1 Sweet Potato, peeled and finely diced (Kumara or Purple Sweet Potato)
1 Parsnip, peeled and finely diced
1 Smoked Ham Hock, trimmed of fat **or 2 Hocks = 2.5 kilograms**
8 Cups of Water **or 12 cups to cover Hocks**
1 Bay Leaf
McKenzie's Pepper Grinder to taste

METHOD:

1. Wash green split peas and pick over to remove any discoloured peas and any other matter.
2. Heat oil in a large pot and sauté onion and garlic for 2 minutes. Add all remaining ingredients to the pot. Cover and simmer for approximately 2-2 ½ hours or until thickened, stirring occasionally.
3. Remove hock and prepare by removing the skins and all visible fat. Dice the lean ham and set aside. Discard bay leaf from soup.
4. Puree soup in a food processor or blender. Or if you prefer a thicker soup, use a potato masher to slightly mash the vegetables. (Step 10) (This is Optional).
5. Add diced ham back to soup and stir through.
6. Season to taste with pepper.

God's Pharmacy
Cholesterol
Anti-Cancer Foods

Special Health Foods

Small Potatoes = 30 minutes

Squash = 20 minutes

Broccolli = 5 to 10 minutes

Carrots = 15 minutes

Cooking with Shea

DANNY'S DELICIOUS SALAD

Onions

Carrots

Red Salmon

Beetroot

Asparagus

Bread

Lettuce

Cheese

White Review: Evans Tate Classic White 2010 & Mushroom & White Wine Risotto

Winery: Evans & Tate

Wine Region: South West Australia

Grapes: Chardonnay, Sauvignon Blanc & Semillion
Recommended Food Pairings:
Chardonnay will pair well with poultry dishes, pork, seafood or recipes that have a heavy cream or butter base. Also consider pairing unoaked Chardonnay with guacamole, garlic, salads, grilled shrimp or even curry dishes.

My Verdict: 3/5

Tasting Notes:

Zesty start with a smooth finish. Lime aromas with crisp apple highlighted towards the end. The Sauv Blanc grapes definitely help ease into this Chardonnay.

Pairing Thoughts:

I very much enjoyed the wine with my Man-Pleasing Chicken & a side of Mushroom & Rosemary Risotto (which I added a splash of the wine to) it was a great pairing particularly with the creamy cheese in the risotto. I think it would definitely be a great wine to highlight avocado in any meal or salad.

Cooking with Shea

Mushroom & Rosemary Risotto (Modified by HOTD)

Source

Ingredients:

1.25L (4 cups) water
- 2 vegetable or chicken stock cubes, crumbled (see note)
- 1 tbs olive oil
- 1 brown onion, finely chopped
- 1 tbs fresh rosemary leaves, chopped
- 200g small button mushrooms, quartered
- 100g Swiss brown mushrooms, sliced
- 330g (1 1/2 cups) arborio rice
- 1 tbs fresh lemon juice
- 40g (1/2 cup) shredded parmesan
- 1/3 cup chopped fresh continental parsley
- 2 cloves of garlic
- 1 cup of white wine

Method:

1. Bring water, wine and stock cubes to the boil in a saucepan over medium heat. Reduce heat to low. Hold at a gentle simmer.
2. Heat the oil in a large saucepan over medium heat. Add the onion & garlic and cook, stirring, for 2 minutes or until soft. Add the rosemary and combined mushroom, and cook, stirring, for 3 minutes or until the mushroom is soft.
3. Add the rice and cook, stirring, for 1 minute or until the grains appear glassy. Add a ladleful (about 125ml/1/2 cup) of the simmering stock to the rice mixture and stir with a wooden spoon until the liquid is absorbed. Add the stock, a ladleful at a time, stirring constantly and allowing liquid to be absorbed before adding the next ladleful. Continue for 25 minutes or until rice is just tender and risotto is creamy.
4. Stir in the lemon juice, and half the parmesan and half the parsley. Top with remaining parmesan and remaining parsley.

Cooking with Shea

GLAZED HAM

Most people prefer buying a cooked leg of ham and glazing it themselves about an hour before serving time. All of the following glazes can be made up to a week before using and stored, covered, in the refrigerator; none is suitable to freeze. Ham itself can be frozen for up to 8 weeks but should be glazed just before baking.

8kg cooked leg of ham
whole cloves

Make a decorative cut through ham rind about 10cm from shank end of leg; run thumb under edge of rind at other end of leg then, using fingers to loosen it, pull rind away from the fat. Continue to carefully pull rind away from fat until you reach decorative cut at shank end; discard rind.

Make shallow cuts in one direction diagonally across fat at 2cm intervals then shallow cut diagonally in opposite direction, forming diamonds. Do not cut through surface of top fat or fat will spread, losing pattern, during cooking. Place 1 clove in centre of each diamond then position ham on wire rack in large baking dish. Wrap shank with foil; brush ham with glaze.

Bake, uncovered, in moderate oven about 50 minutes or until browned all over, brushing frequently with glaze during cooking.

MAPLE SYRUP GLAZE

1 tablespoon mustard powder
1½ cups (375ml) maple-flavoured syrup
⅓ cup (80ml) cider vinegar

Mix all ingredients in small bowl until powder dissolves.

REDCURRANT JELLY AND ORANGE GLAZE

½ cup (125ml) redcurrant jelly
¼ cup (60ml) port
½ cup (125ml) orange juice
½ cup (125ml) marmalade

Mix all ingredients in small pan; stir over low heat until jelly and marmalade melt. Simmer 5 minutes or until mixture thickens slightly.

MANGO GLAZE

⅔ cup (160ml) mango nectar
⅓ cup (80ml) mango chutney
¼ cup (50g) firmly packed brown sugar
1 tablespoon Dijon mustard

Mix all ingredients in small pan; stir over low heat until chutney melts.

APRICOT GLAZE

⅔ cup (160ml) apricot nectar
⅓ cup (80ml) apricot jam
¼ cup (50g) firmly packed brown sugar
1 tablespoon Dijon mustard

Mix all ingredients in small pan; stir over low heat until jam melts.

SWEET CHILLI GLAZE

⅓ cup (80ml) mild sweet chilli sauce
¼ cup (60ml) lime juice
2 teaspoons finely grated fresh ginger
2 tablespoons teriyaki sauce

Mix all ingredients in small bowl.

BARBECUE HONEY GLAZE

¼ cup (60ml) barbecue sauce
¼ cup (60ml) Worcestershire sauce
¼ cup (60ml) tomato sauce
¼ cup (60ml) honey

Mix all ingredients in small pan; stir over low heat until honey melts.

CLOCKWISE FROM TOP: Redcurrant Jelly and Orange Glaze; Apricot Glaze; Barbecue Honey Glaze; Mango Glaze. CENTRE: Sweet Chilli Glaze.

11 TASTY POTATO DISHES

Roasted Potato Medley

This trio of potatoes, drizzled with olive oil and fresh herbs, are oven-roasted for a crispy outside and a creamy smooth inside – delicious!

Cooking with Shea

Roasted Potato Medley

Prep Time **15 mins** Cook Time **25 mins**

Ingredients
SERVES 4

- 2 sweet potatoes
- 4 yellow-fleshed potatoes, such as Bintje
- 8 new potatoes
- ¼ cup plus 2 tbsp olive oil
- 1 tsp dried tarragon
- ⅛ tsp salt
- ⅛ tsp black pepper

Easy Step-by-Step

1. Preheat oven to 210°C/425°F. Peel and cube the sweet potatoes and yellow-fleshed potatoes. Scrub the new potatoes and cut into cubes.

2. Place the potatoes in a large saucepan. Add enough lightly salted water to cover the potatoes. Bring to the boil and cook the potatoes for 3 minutes. Drain thoroughly.

3. Spread the potatoes in a single layer on a large nonstick baking sheet.

4. Drizzle the potatoes with olive oil and sprinkle with tarragon, salt and pepper. Roast potatoes until browned and crisp, about 25 minutes. Serve immediately.

SERVING SUGGESTION

This crispy potato dish is the perfect complement to roast chicken or pork. Serve with a caesar salad to round out the meal.

Great Ideas

For extra flavour, cook 4 whole leeks in boiling water for 7–10 minutes until just tender. Drain and chop; add in Step 2.

Instead of the tarragon, you can use 1 teaspoon each dried thyme and dried rosemary.

Nutritional information per serving: kilojoules 1684/calories 401, fat 14.4g (sat fat 2g), carbs 64.6g

© MMVII International Masters Publishers AB. Mealtimes Made Easy. AU C600 20000/2

Cooking with Shea

Salad Niçoise

Preparation 20 mins | Cooking 20 mins | Serves 4

This simple salad is perfect for a quick weeknight dinner.

300g green beans, trimmed
600g small new potatoes
6 ripe tomatoes, cut into wedges
425g can tuna in oil, drained and roughly flaked
4 hard-boiled eggs, peeled and halved lengthways
½ cup Kalamata olives
Mustard cress or micro-herbs, to serve (optional)

Red wine dressing
¼ cup extra virgin olive oil
1 tbs red wine vinegar
½ tsp caster sugar

STEP 1 Bring a large saucepan of water to the boil over high heat. Add beans and cook for 2 minutes until just crisp and vibrant. Remove beans with a slotted spoon, refresh in cold water and pat dry. Set beans aside. Add potatoes to pan and bring the water back to the boil. Gently boil potatoes for 10-15 minutes (depending on size) until just tender. Drain and refresh in cold water until cold. Set aside in a colander to dry then halve potatoes.

STEP 2 To make dressing, combine all ingredients in a screw-top jar. Season with salt and pepper to taste. Shake until well combined.

STEP 3 Arrange beans, potatoes, tomatoes, tuna, eggs and olives in serving bowls. Drizzle with dressing, sprinkle with mustard cress or micro-herbs if using and serve.

Good for you... TOMATOES

Tomatoes are the richest food source of lycopene, a member of the carotenoid family which is important for the health of the prostate gland. The redder the tomato, the higher its lycopene content.

SYDNEY MARKETS For more fresh fruit & veg recipes visit www.sydneymarkets.com.au

Cooking with Shea

Roast pumpkin
with pearl couscous & pomegranate

Prep: 15 mins | **Cook:** 35 mins | **Serves:** 4

INGREDIENTS

1.2kg whole butternut pumpkin
2 tbs olive oil
2 tbs dukkah
1 tbs honey
1 garlic clove, crushed
250g pearl couscous
¼ cup sultanas
½ cup coriander, chopped
4 spring onions, chopped
⅓ cup pistachios, chopped
1 pomegranate, ¼ cup arils removed

Lemon dressing

2 tbs olive oil
1 tbs apple cider vinegar
1 tbs finely chopped preserved lemon

METHOD

1. Preheat oven to 200°C.
2. Trim ends from pumpkin. Slice into 2cm-thick slices and lay into a roasting pan. Rub with 1 tbs oil and sprinkle with dukkah. Roast for 20 minutes. Drizzle with honey and roast for another 15 minutes or until tender and golden.
3. Meanwhile, heat remaining oil in a saucepan. Add garlic, couscous and sultanas. Stir to coat with oil. Pour in 2½ cups boiling water. Cover, reduce heat to low and simmer, stirring twice during cooking, for 10 minutes. Transfer to a bowl. Cool. Add coriander, onion and pistachios. Toss through to combine.
4. To make the dressing, combine oil, vinegar and lemon. Pour over couscous mixture and toss through. Set aside.
5. Remove pumpkin from roasting pan. Remove and discard seeds and skin. Dice flesh and add to couscous mixture. Serve topped with pomegranate arils.

For more Easter inspiration visit woolworths.com.au/easter-recipes

On show 14/3/18 – 2/4/18_NAT

CHOLESTEROL

EAT

EAT SMALL SERVINGS OF RED MEAT

EAT CHICKEN AND OILY FISH MORE OFTEN

EAT A SERVING OF STARCHY FOOD SUCH AS
POTATOES, PASTA, RICE AT EACH MEAL

EAT AT LEAST FIVE PORTIONS OF FRUIT AND VEGETABLES A DAY

EAT LOTS OF FIBRE
PORRIDGE, BEANS, PEAS, PULSES, FRUIT AND VEGETABLES

EAT FRESH PRODUCE RATHER THAN PROCESSED

EAT PLENTY OF OILY FISH, SARDINES, SALMON, TROUT, FRESH TUNA
FULL OF OMEGA 3 FATS FOR A HEALTHY HEART.

CHOOSE

CHOOSE FISH OR LEAN MEAT INSTEAD OF RED MEAT

BE

BE MORE PHYSICALLY ACTIVE

USE

USE HERBS, SPICES, LEMONS OR GARLIC TO FLAVOUR FOOD

USE OILS SUCH AS – OLIVE, CANOLA, PEANUT, FISH OILS

USE POLYUNSATURATED MARGARINE

AVOID

SUGARY FOODS AND SALT
SATURATED FATS – ANIMAL FATS, MEAT, EGGS,
DIARY PRODUCTS, BUTTER, CHEESE, FATTY MEATS.

CUT DOWN ON

CHEESE, PASTRIES, BISCUITS, MARGARINE, OILS, SUGARS, FATS

LIMIT

ALCOHOL AS IT IS HIGH IN CALORIES

GOOD FATS

UNSATURATED FATS ARE USUALLY PLANT AND FISH OILS

BAD FATS

SATURATED FATS ARE FOUND IN –
ANIMAL FATS, MEAT, EGGS, DIARY PRODUCTS, BUTTER, CHEESE, FATTY MEATS

FACTS ABOUT FATS

SATURATED FATS RAISE CHOLESTEROL

UNSATURATED FATS ARE NOT THOUGHT TO RAISE BLOO CHOLESTEROL AND MAY LOWER LEVELS

LACTOSE INTOLERANCE

USE AGED CHEESES
YOGHURT BREAKS DOWN LACTOSE

Anti Cancer Foods

GREEN LEAFY FOODS
KALE – CHARD – LEMON – GINGER
BROCCOLLI – LETTUCE – CABBAGE
BEANS
TOMATOES
FLAXSEED OIL

SALMON
EGGS

GARLIC
WALNUTS

ROSEMARY – OREGANO – CLOVES – ANISEED
CHICKEN SOUP FOR INFLUENZA
APPLE CIDER VINEGAR

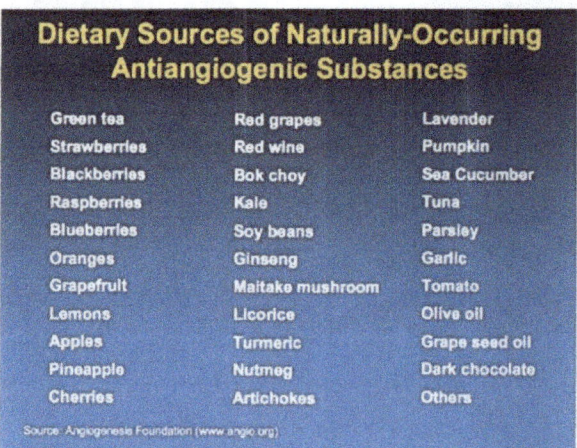

AntiCancer Foods

Proponents of the acid-alkaline theory of disease and nutrition maintain that eating too much meat, dairy, poultry, fish, eggs and dairy, which are all acid-forming foods, disrupts the body's delicate pH balance. When your body has to work too hard to rid itself of excess acid, it also loses valuable minerals through your urine, leading to fatigue and possibly illness. However, critics of the acid-alkaline theory say that your body knows how to balance pH on its own, and excess acid buildup in the body is only temporary.

Diseases Thrive in an ACIDIC Environment

Scientists report that over 150 or more degenerative diseases are caused by high acid levels!! Parasites, viruses, bad bacteria, and disease cannot live in an alkaline body.

Body fluids range between 4.5 and 7.5 pH (blood must maintain 7.35 to 7.45 pH). A 1-point drop on the pH scale is 10 times more acidic - from 7 to 6 is 10 times, from 7 to 5 is 100 times, from 7 to 2 is 100,000 times more acidic.

Therefore: Eat more Alkalizing foods and Less Acidic Foods

Cooking with Shea

ALKALIZING FOODS

VEGETABLES
- Garlic
- Asparagus
- Fermented Veggies
- Watercress
- Beets
- Broccoli
- Brussel sprouts
- Cabbage
- Carrot
- Cauliflower
- Celery
- Chard
- Chlorella
- Collard Greens
- Cucumber
- Eggplant
- Kale
- Kohlrabi
- Lettuce
- Mushrooms
- Mustard Greens
- Dulce
- Dandelions
- Edible Flowers
- Onions
- Parsnips (high glycemic)
- Peas
- Peppers
- Pumpkin
- Rutabaga
- Sea Veggies
- Spirulina
- Sprouts
- Squashes
- Alfalfa
- Barley Grass
- Wheat Grass
- Wild Greens
- Nightshade Veggies

FRUITS
- Apple
- Apricot
- Avocado
- Banana (high glycemic)
- Cantaloupe
- Cherries
- Currants
- Dates/Figs
- Grapes
- Grapefruit
- Lime
- Honeydew Melon
- Nectarine
- Orange
- Lemon
- Peach
- Pear
- Pineapple
- All Berries
- Tangerine
- Tomato
- Tropical Fruits
- Watermelon

PROTEIN
- Eggs
- Whey Protein Powder
- Cottage Cheese
- Chicken Breast
- Yogurt
- Almonds
- Chestnuts
- Tofu (fermented)
- Flax Seeds
- Pumpkin Seeds
- Tempeh (fermented)
- Squash Seeds
- Sunflower Seeds
- Millet
- Sprouted Seeds
- Nuts

OTHER
- Apple Cider Vinegar
- Bee Pollen
- Lecithin Granules
- Probiotic Cultures
- Green Juices
- Veggies Juices
- Fresh Fruit Juice
- Organic Milk (unpasteurized)
- Mineral Water
- Alkaline Antioxidant Water
- Green Tea
- Herbal Tea
- Dandelion Tea
- Ginseng Tea
- Banchi Tea
- Kombucha

SWEETENERS
- Stevia

SPICES/SEASONINGS
- Cinnamon
- Curry
- Ginger
- Mustard
- Chili Pepper
- Sea Salt
- Miso
- Tamari
- All Herbs

ORIENTAL VEGETABLES
- Maitake
- Daikon
- Dandelion Root
- Shitake
- Kombu
- Reishi
- Nori
- Umeboshi
- Wakame
- Sea Veggies

Cooking with Shea

ACIDIFYING FOODS

FATS & OILS
Avocado Oil
Canola Oil
Corn Oil
Hemp Seed Oil
Flax Oil
Lard
Olive Oil
Safflower Oil
Sesame Oil
Sunflower Oil

FRUITS
Cranberries

GRAINS
Rice Cakes
Wheat Cakes
Amaranth
Barley
Buckwheat
Corn
Oats (rolled)
Quinoi
Rice (all)
Rye
Spelt
Kamut
Wheat
Hemp Seed Flour

DAIRY
Cheese, Cow
Cheese, Goat
Cheese, Processed
Cheese, Sheep
Milk
Butter

NUTS & BUTTERS
Cashews
Brazil Nuts
Peanuts
Peanut Butter
Pecans
Tahini
Walnuts

ANIMAL PROTEIN
Beef
Carp
Clams
Fish
Lamb
Lobster
Mussels
Oyster
Pork
Rabbit
Salmon
Shrimp
Scallops
Tuna
Turkey
Venison

PASTA (WHITE)
Noodles
Macaroni
Spaghetti

OTHER
Distilled Vinegar
Wheat Germ
Potatoes

DRUGS & CHEMICALS
Chemicals
Drugs, Medicinal
Drugs, Psychedelic
Pesticides
Herbicides

ALCOHOL
Beer
Spirits
Hard Liquor
Wine

BEANS & LEGUMES
Black Beans
Chick Peas
Green Peas
Kidney Beans
Lentils
Lima Beans
Pinto Beans
Red Beans
Soy Beans
Soy Milk
White Beans
Rice Milk
Almond Milk

Anti-Inflammatory Foods

1. <u>Kelp</u> contains fucoidan, a type of complex carbohydrate that is anti-inflammatory, anti-tumor and anti-oxidative.

2. <u>Turmeric</u> contains a powerful, non-toxic compound called curcumin. Studies show that turmeric's anti-inflammatory effects are on a par with potent drugs such as hydrocortisone and Motrin, but yet having none of their side effects

3. <u>Salmon</u> contains EPA (eicosapentaenoic acid) and DHA (docosahexaenoic acid), two potent omega-3 fatty acids that douse inflammation. T

4. <u>Shiitake Mushrooms</u> contain compounds that lower cholesterol, enhance immune function and reduce risk of several kinds of cancer.

5. <u>Green Tea</u> contains flavonoids that are potent natural anti-inflammatory compounds that have been shown in numerous studies to reduce the risk of heart disease and cancer.

Other Anti Inflammatory Foods are: Papaya, Blueberries, Extra Virgin Olive Oil, Brocolli, Sweet Potato,

<u>Foods to Avoid:</u> Sugar, common vegetable oils, dairy products, red and processed meats, alcohol, refined grains, food additives like aspartame and MSG, trans fats,

http://eatingmywaytobetterhealth.blogspot.com/

Dietary Fibre Guide

Include foods rich in dietary fibre in your daily diet to ensure you maintain regularity. Remember the average daily requirement is around 30g.

Food	Serving Size	Soluble	Insoluble	Total
Fruits				
Pear, fresh, unpeeled	1 medium	0.7	3.9	4.6
Dates, dried	3	0.1	4.2	4.3
Avocado	½	1.2	2.6	3.8
Prunes, dried	5	1.1	2.0	3.1
Apple, unpeeled	1 medium	0.4	2.6	3.0
Orange, fresh	1 medium	0.5	1.7	2.2
Blueberries, fresh or frozen	½ cup	0.2	1.9	2.1
Banana	1 medium	0.5	1.3	1.8
Peach, fresh, unpeeled	1	0.6	1.1	1.7
Raisins, seedless	¼ cup	0.2	1.4	1.6
Papaya, fresh, cubed	½ cup	0.1	1.4	1.5
Kiwi Fruit	1 medium	0.3	1.2	1.5
Strawberries	½ cup	0.3	1.0	1.3
Pineapple, diced	½ cup	0.1	0.6	0.7
Cantaloupe, fresh, cubed	½ cup	0.1	0.5	0.6
Grapes	10	tr	0.5	0.5
Watermelon, fresh, cubed	½ cup	tr	0.3	0.3
Vegetables				
Potato, white, unpeeled	1 medium	1.0	3.1	4.1
Brussel sprouts	½ cup	0.4	2.8	3.2
Spinach, raw	2 cups	0.3	2.0	2.3
Potato, white, peeled	1 medium	0.4	1.7	2.1
Carrot, sliced	½ cup	0.4	1.5	1.9
Broccoli, cooked or raw	2 stalks	0.2	1.7	1.8
Asparagus, canned or fresh	½ cup	0.3	1.4	1.7
Corn, whole kernel	½ cup	0.1	1.5	1.6
Potato salad, peeled	½ cup	0.4	1.1	1.5
Beans, cooked or raw	½ cup	0.3	1.2	1.5
Onion, raw, chopped	½ cup	0.1	1.1	1.2
Cauliflower, cooked or raw	½ cup	0.2	1.0	1.2
Potato, french fries	10 strips	0.2	0.9	1.1
Celery, diced, cooked or raw	½ cup	0.1	1.0	1.1
Pepper, green or chilli, chopped	½ cup	0.1	0.8	0.9
Tomato, canned or fresh	½ cup	0.2	0.6	0.8
Bean sprouts	½ cup	tr	0.8	0.8
Lettuce, fresh, shredded	1 cup	tr	0.7	0.7
Cucumber, unpeeled	½ cup	tr	0.5	0.5
Mushrooms, fresh, pieces	½ cup	0.1	0.2	0.3
Legumes				
Beans, kidney, canned	½ cup	1.0	3.5	4.5
Peas, green, canned or frozen	½ cup	0.3	2.8	3.1
Lentils	½ cup	0.1	2.8	2.9
Nuts & Seeds				
Almonds, roasted with skin	22 whole	0.1	2.4	2.5
Peanuts	30-40 whole	0.1	1.9	1.9
Cashews, roasted	18 medium	0.1	1.2	1.3
Pumpkin seeds	1 tbsp	tr	0.7	0.8
Popcorn	1 cup	tr	0.8	0.8
Grain Products				
Cereal, All Bran	½ cup	0.7	7.4	8.1
Wheat germ	¼ cup	0.3	3.6	3.9
Bread, whole wheat	1 slice	0.3	2.2	2.5
Pasta, macaroni, spaghetti etc	1 cup	0.4	1.6	2.0
Muffin, English	1	0.3	1.3	1.7
Noodles, Chow Mein	1 cup	0.4	1.1	1.5
Cereal, cornflakes	1 cup	0.1	1.1	1.2
Bun, hamburger	1	0.3	0.7	1.0
Bread roll, hard	1 small	0.2	0.6	0.8
Pancake, 10 cm diameter	2	0.2	0.7	0.8
Bread, white or Italian	1 slice	0.2	0.6	0.8
Taco Shell	1	tr	0.7	0.7
Cereal, Special K	1 cup	0.1	0.7	0.7
Bread, rye	1 slice	0.2	0.5	0.7
Rice, cooked	½ cup	tr	0.3	0.4
Cookies, shortbread	4	0.2	0.3	0.4
Doughnut, plain	1	0.1	0.2	0.3
Crackers, saltine	4	0.1	0.2	0.3
Ice cream cone, Cornet Cup	1	tr	0.1	0.1

tr=trace. Less than 0.05 g (fresh weight) per serving

Any difference between the sum of the soluble and insoluble fibre and total fibre is due to rounding of data.

Fibre values have been calculated according to the Uppsala method extracted from Marlett JA, Cheung T-F: Database and quick methods of assessing typical dietary fiber intakes using data for 228 commonly consumed foods. Copyright by the American Dietetic Association. Reprinted with permission from the Journal of the American Dietetic Association, 1997; Vol.97;10,1139-1148.

Normacol® plus sterculia 62% frangula bark 8%

Normafibe® sterculia 62%

June Fresh: The bounty of fresh winter vegetables

Janne Ramsay

Translator

Did you know the best nutritionist in the world is you? Why? Because Because it means you are taking responsibility for your own health. Think about such health issues as why there is an increase in cancer, or why the number of people with cardiovascular disease or arthritis is increasing?

Eating fresh and making the right food choices is essential to good health.

What's fresh and in season in June?

Did you know fruit offers a colour rainbow of nutrients?

Apples	Avocados	Banana	Custard apples
Grapefruit	Kiwifruit	Lemons	Mandarins
Nashi	Oranges – Navel	Passionfruit	Pears
Pomelo	Quince	Rhubarb	

Did you know that fresh vegetables provide nutrients that can help your body live younger?

Beetroot	Broccoli	Brussels sprouts	Cabbage
Carrots	Cauliflower	Celeriac	Celery
Fennel	Jerusalem artichokes	Kohlrabi	Leeks
Olives	Onions	Parsnips	Potatoes
Pumpkin	Silverbeet	Spinach	Swede
Sweet potato	Turnips		

What is exciting about winter vegetables?

When we think of winter vegetables we think of winter soups and roasted vegetables. Typical root vegetables in a roast have a starch structure. These vegetables are better cooked to open up the starch structure and allow for easier digestion.

How to get the best flavours from your Roasted Winter Vegetables

- Pre-heat your over to 200°/180° Celsius/fan-forced.

Cooking with Shea

- A combination of roast vegetables such as potato, sweet potato, pumpkin, carrots, parsnips and red onions served with a plate of leafy greens provides a rainbow of colour.
- Wash vegetables in cold running water and gently scrub with a vegetable brush.
- Prepare vegetables by cutting into chunky bite sized pieces and follow by drying well.
- Toss in olive oil, sprinkle with Himalayan Sea Salt and ground pepper. For extra flavour consider your favourite herb such as fresh rosemary, fresh thyme, organic turmeric or sprinkle with Vogel Herbamare.
- Vegetables should be spread in a single layer in a large baking pan.
- To add extra crispiness, increase oven to 220° Celsius/fan-forced for the last 5 minutes of cooking.

What nutrients can I get from a plate of roasted fresh root vegetables?

Sweet potatoes – are rich in carotenes, the darker the sweet potato the higher the concentration. They are also a good source of dietary fibre as well as Vitamin C and Vitamin B6 as well as manganese, biotin, copper, vitamin B5, vitamin B2 and dietary fibre. Sweet potatoes should be firm and are best stored in a dark, well ventilated, for up to 10 days.

Potatoes – often misunderstood the potato is a source of potassium, vitamin C, vitamin B6, vitamin B3 and dietary fibre. Potatoes should be fresh and firm and should be stored in a cool, dark, dry place. If stored at too high temperature you will notice the potatoes sprout and dehydrate. Avoid potatoes with green coloration as this may indicate the presence of solanine which is toxic.

Parsnips – add extra flavour to a plate of root vegetables and are rich in nutrients including folic acid, vitamin C, vitamin B5, manganese, copper as well as vitamin B1, vitamin B3, magnesium and potassium. Fresh parsnips are available most of the year but the winter crops harvested in spring are higher in natural sugars. Look for parsnips that are firm and well-shaped. They can be stored in the fridge for up to two weeks.

Pumpkin – the rich orange colour of pumpkins is a good indication of the rich source of carotene they provide. Pumpkins provide dietary fibre and are a good source of vitamin C, vitamin B1, folic acid and potassium. Pumpkin can be stored for one to three months depending on how fresh it is when purchased. Look for any signs of decay before buying. Store in a dark, dry place. Once the pumpkin as been cut it needs to be wrapped and stored in the refrigerator and will last for one to two days.

Carrots – another rich orange vegetable, carrots are a rich source of carotene and have many health benefits which will be highlighted in our July seasonal fruit and vegetable guide.

Turnips – are also a good source of dietary fibre. They are a good source in many nutrients including vitamin C, vitamin B5, manganese, copper, folic acid as well as providing a source of vitamin B1, vitamin B2, vitamin B3, vitamin B6, vitamin E, magnesium and potassium. Turnips should be firm and smooth with no signs of decay. They are best stored in the refrigerator in a perforated plastic bag.

Onions – are a good source of vitamin C, vitamin B6, chromium, biotin and dietary fibre. Select onions that are hard with smooth, dry skin. They can be stored in a well-ventilated place at room temperature away from direct light.

Ask a Naturopath…

Cooking with Shea

Mr Vitamins Naturopath and Nutritionist, Janne Ramsay is passionate about re-educating people on selecting and buying seasonally fresh fruit and vegetables and rediscovering their taste. If you are interested in how much nutrition you are getting out of your diet, Janne can provide you with a full dietary analysis…..

Mr Vitamins Naturopath, **Janne Ramsay** is passionate about re-educating people on selecting and buying seasonally fresh fruit and vegetables and rediscovering their taste. If you are interested in how much nutrition you are getting out of your diet, Janne can provide you with a full dietary analysis…..

Learn more about
Naturopath Janne Ramsay here…

Other Mr Vitamins related posts:

Is Organic Food Worth A Higher Price?
Can you trust what a food label tells you?
Is your fresh food really fresh?
The Lunchbox Revolution
Do you know how to get your recommended daily Calcium?
Glyphosate: What Is it? Where is it? Why we should care

Cooking with Shea

Cooking with Shea

It's been said that God first separated the salt water
from the fresh, made dry land, planted a garden,
made animals and fish...
All before making a human.
He made and provided what we'd need before we were born.
These are best & more powerful when eaten raw.
We're such slow learners...
God left us a great clue as to what foods help what
part of our body!
God's Pharmacy! Amazing!

A sliced carrot looks like a human eye.
The pupil, iris and radiating lines look just
like the human eye.
And YES, science now shows carrots greatly
enhance blood flow and function of the eyes.

Cooking with Shea

*A tomato has four chambers and is red.
The heart has four chambers and is red.
All the research shows that tomatoes are loaded with
lycopine and are indeed pure heart and blood food.*

*A walnut looks like a little brain, with a left and right
hemisphere, upper cerebrums and lower cerebellums.
Even the wrinkles or folds on the nut are just like the
neo-cortex. We now know that walnuts help develop more
than three dozen neuron-transmitters for brain function.*

Grapes hang in a cluster that has the shape of a heart. Each grape looks like a blood cell and all of the research today shows that grapes are also profound heart and blood vitalising food.

Kidney Beans actually heal and help maintain kidney functions and yes, they actually look exactly like the human kidneys.

Cooking with Shea

Celery, Bok Choy, Rhubarb and many more look just like bones.
These foods specifically target bone strength.

Bones are 23% sodium and these foods are 23% sodium.
If you don't have enough sodium in your diet,
the body pulls it from the bones, thus making them weak.
These foods replenish the skeletal needs of the body.

Figs are full of seeds and hang in twos when they grow.
Figs increase the mobility of male sperm and increase
the numbers of Sperm as well to overcome male sterility.

Cooking with Shea

Onions look like the body's cells. Today's research shows onions help clear waste materials from all of the body cells. They even produce tears which wash the epithelial layers of the eyes. A working companion, Garlic, also helps eliminate waste materials and dangerous free radicals from the body.

Oranges, Grapefruits and other Citrus fruits look just like the mammary glands of the female and actually assist the health of the breasts and the movement of lymph in and out of the breasts.

Cooking with Shea

Avocadoes, Eggplant and Pears target the health and function of the womb and cervix of the female - they look just like these organs. Today's research shows that when a woman eats one avocado a week, it balances hormones, sheds unwanted birth weight, and prevents cervical cancers. And how profound is this? It takes exactly nine (9) months to grow an avocado from blossom to ripened fruit There are over 14,000 photolytic chemical constituents of nutrition in each one of these foods (modern science has only studied and named about 141 of them).

Olives assist the health and function of the ovaries

Cooking with Shea

Sweet Potatoes look like the pancreas and actually balance the glycemic index of diabetics.

www.ingramcontent.com/pod-product-compliance
Lightning Source LLC
Chambersburg PA
CBHW081420300426
44110CB00016BA/2330